The Children's God

The
Children's God

David Heller

The University of Chicago Press   *Chicago and London*

DAVID HELLER, a psychologist, is the author of
Power in Psychotherapeutic Practice and coedi-
tor, with Daniel Goleman, of *The Pleasures of
Psychology.* Currently, he is completing *The
Male Image*, a study of what constitutes mascu-
linity.

The University of Chicago Press, Chicago 60637
The University of Chicago Press, Ltd., London
© 1986 by The University of Chicago
All rights reserved. Published 1986
Printed in the United States of America

95 94 93 92 91 90 89 88 87 86   54321

Library of Congress Cataloging-in-Publication Data

Heller, David.
    The children's God.

    Bibliography: p.
    Includes index.
    1. God. 2. Children--Religious life. I. Title.
BT102.H43 1986   231   85-24581
ISBN 0-226-32635-7

*For all thoughtful
friends under
the age of
twelve*

Contents

Preface

Notoriously, book prefaces can be quite tedious. Books concerning religion and psychology are far from exceptions to this rule. But I ask the reader to bear with me and read carefully, because I strongly believe that *The Children's God* is best understood in light of some very specific intentions.

Above all, I wish to depict the many dimensions of deity imagery in children of ages four to twelve; at the same time, I want to create a portrait of the several potential influences that shape these deity representations. The book is thus primarily illustrative rather than conclusive. In no way is it a definitive word on the state of religious belief. The God concept, or its absence, may well have a special place in the imaginative realm of the child. If I have drawn some or much of the child's fantasy terrain and discovered something common about the functions of a deity image, then I would consider this exploration most successful.

My methodological choices follow naturally from this descriptive purpose. So do their limitations. I have elected a broad-sweeping collection approach to fantasy assessment, rather than a precise, finely measured approach. This preference means that my findings are not evidence per se for all children. Rather, the results are guideposts and substantive indicators of where children's common and different ideas are likely to be observed. The benefits of my approach are in the breadth of imagery presented and in the close, individualized understanding of each child as a whole and spiritual person. Yet in no way can I assuredly claim to have captured the child's relationship with a real God. If after conducting the study I still maintain a sense of awe, it should not be surprising. The mystery of the child's view of transcendence is not likely to be portrayed fully by a single study or discussion.

The words and images of the forty children that enliven these pages present clear theological perspectives, often in fresh and unpredictable language and form. Children have their own kind of style and grace; perhaps after reading about their personal searches you may feel that about a religious "grace" as well.

The letters that open chapters 1, 2, and 4 are taken from Eric Marshall and Stuart Hample's *More Children's Letters to God* (New York: Simon and Schuster, 1967). The letters that begin chapters 3, 5, 7, and 9 appear in Marshall and Hample's earlier volume, *Children's Letters to God* (New York: Simon and Schuster, 1966). The letter in chapter 6 is taken from *Dear God Kids* (New York: Intercontinental Imports, 1983). The letter that begins chapter 10 is my own.

Introduction: Children's Conceptions

Dear God,
  I read your book and I like it. Did you
write any others? I would like to write a book
someday with the same kind of stories.
Where did you get your ideas?

Best wishes,
Mark

When I overhear a parent turning deaf to the heartfelt expressions of a child, or even scoffing at the child's belief, I remind myself that I too have been guilty— guilty of not taking children's communications seriously enough. I also remind myself of the lovely and quietly resounding words of C. Madelaine Dixon, as she writes concerning the child's quest for meaning, and sometimes, the child's search for a God:

> Each child must plumb vastness and infinity. Let him call it what he will—fire, water, death, God, worlds, stars. And somehow he must share his curiosity and his awe before he has formed many static answers. . . . We forget that the probing of strange phenomena, creation, God, death, magic, has made our scientists, our artists, our religious leaders, throughout the ages. Why should we shorten this probing or cover it up for children? (1930, 37)

Children's religious explorations, and the early life-course influences which may determine their inner travels, are the prevailing concerns of this book. Essentially, I am interested in children's conceptions of God. These "conceptions" refer to the imagery, thoughts, and feelings which crystallize to make up the characters of the child's inner world. I am particularly interested in this inner world, a domain that exists beyond surface responses and the wish for adult approval. It is in such a location that the most colorful and passionate characters live with the child—the mythological abode of Superman and Wonder Woman, for certain, but perhaps also the home of Adam and Eve and Jesus.

In speaking of "God," I mean to concentrate upon the special god or deity of each child, however unique or uniform such representations might be. I am not so much concerned with what the children may call their representations, which may vary from names like "Lord" to descriptions like "my friend." I have a tremendous investment, however, in discovering the major, unifying image that accompanies these titles. What most matters, it seems to me, is what the child feels is central and crucial in his or her own life. Such clear importance is the ultimate criterion for a child's God. In asking the children to share their conceptions, I tried as much as possible to keep the interviews free of my own religious imagery. After all, I wanted to create an atmosphere in which the children could speak freely.

How shall the children speak, I wondered? I suppose this is a question right out of a passage from Psalms or a parable from Matthew, and yet it is also a most relevant inquiry for a sincere appreciation of children's deity conceptions. Originally, I hoped to ask the children to choose their own mode of expression without my suggestion, but trial interview experiences indicated that the children would require a bit of interview structure gently administered. One observation was patently clear: the children seemed to enjoy their greatest freedom of expression within the familiar ambience of a most sanctified children's ritual—the many varieties of play.

To state the obvious, play was natural. In preliminary talks, the children's faces lit up with glee and they responded with alacrity during play-oriented activities. Play was an excellent vehicle for entrance into their inner worlds and its characters. It was through play and discussion that they could portray their human idols, their Larry Birds and their Christie Brinkleys, but also move on from these images to usually less idealized and more personalized deity conceptions. Most memorably, it was within the realms of play and discussion that the children might even acknowledge that they didn't know if, in fact, there was a God. It was in such a free-flowing atmosphere that the children could, perchance, doubt.

The investigative schedule, including drawing, story telling, play scenarios, interviewing, and letters to God, was developed with four focal questions in mind. I felt strongly that these issues would help to organize the children's thematic conceptions:

1. What are children's conceptions of a deity like if we compare the children by religious affiliation? by age? by sex? by personality?
2. What family themes can we observe in these conceptions?
3. Are there themes in these conceptions of a deity that the children manifest in common?
4. Finally, with reference to the implications of children's conceptions, we want to ask, What should parents know about their children's religious conceptions?

While our attention will be placed squarely on these formidable and challenging questions, it will be quite apparent from the outset, I believe, that the children offer insight into topics not thoroughly encompassed by the questions. In living color, the children even develop their own religious questions, as illustrated by the plaintive eight-year-old who, in earnest quest for her own version of the American dream, asked, "Where is the Garden of Eden?"

In their indomitable manner, the forty children whose inner lives unfold on these pages speak refreshingly, their small voices not yet so filtered by the god of expectations that honest moments of desire and fear are edited and deleted. The children speak to questions of faith and doubt, vengeance and power, and justice and love—these same elemental pairings that we adults seem to rally our God representations around. In their simplest phrases and play actions, their lives sometimes offer educational and religious lessons more profound than the prepared curricula and sermons of the adult world. We need to provide a forum for the children to express themselves, and we need to listen to their words with an open, religious heart.

2

The Method: In Search of the Children's God

Dear God,
We were told to write to our favorite
person. I am writing to you even though you
can't write back, 'cause you aren't a person.
But I wanted to write anyway.

Love,
Karen

In my search for the varieties and forms of children's deity representations, I felt it imperative to develop some means of collecting their imagery that would not distort or violate it. Or even worse, I feared, was the possibility that I might fall prey to the unfortunate tendency of psychology to overcategorize such imagery. My primary intention was to enter the inner world of the child and, through this excursion into phenomenology, to gain an insider's appreciation of the deity representations and their personalized meanings. Yet realistically I knew that this would be a difficult undertaking. A ready assortment of questions appeared: How can I get to know the child? How can I encourage the child to be spontaneous? How can I provide an atmosphere safe enough to encourage openness? These were the problems that I encountered, issues which suggested that an orthodox methodology would be insufficient.

Clearly, "something else" was necessary, and something else is what I undertook and am about to describe. I decided that the most important contribution I could make, given the uncharted and relatively neglected nature of the topic in serious discussion, would be a descriptive essay and analysis of what I observed. I would assume the role of an observer-participant, become involved in a real way with the children during the interviews, and report what I observed while carefully considering some factors of socialization that might influence their phenomenal worlds. My choices of psychological instrument, the tools by which I would gently build an alliance and a medium of communication, were elected accordingly. Each was selected to allow the children ample freedom of movement and freedom of thought and, at the same time, to provide a suitable opportunity for comparison and a necessary cohesion to the overall project.

The general approach of semistructured interviews with accompanying prepared tasks has some highly successful precedents in the Pulitzer Prize–winning works of Robert Coles, his *Children of Crisis* series (1964–). Originally interested in the inner struggles of southern black children during desegregation, Coles performed a series of investigations on other special groups of children using their original drawings, stories, and interview responses. In his discussion of method (Coles 1964), maintains that the social science observer is always a participant and that it makes sense to acknowledge this without reservation. In emphasizing the phenomenology of the child, Coles maintains the critical importance of two preparatory concerns: direct observation and question formulation without a priori answers. This seemed like well-informed and sensible advice to me, so I tried to incorporate these considerations into my pursuit.

More recently, educator Valerie Suransky has presented a related approach in *The Erosion of Childhood* (1982). With what she calls a "social phenomenological" foray into the various inhibitory structures of the

American school system, Suransky makes a compelling case for the benefits of phenomenology over more objective approaches. In an investigation with clear implications for the study of children and religion, Suransky employs a thematic analysis of her own observational notes and recordings to parcel out what exactly children are saying about education. Based on her own observational experience, she adopts a radical view concerning the clear importance of being a participant in order to understand. In keeping with this perspective, she notes the importance of inserting oneself in the child's world of play in order to come close to the child. A portion of her argument is phrased in a language that touches coincidentally on the subject of our concern: "The child's open communication with the world is his play. In fact, it is the place wherein the individual's primordial and ordinary relation to being is formed." (Vanden Burgt 1981, 121). Both this social-phenomenological perspective and thematic analysis seemed applicable to a spontaneous activity like play, and both seemed appropriate for a study of spontaneous religion.

Contributing to these methodological precedents was my dawning awareness that I had entered into very special territory in journeying into childhood religion. Flexibility and a method that was adaptable were essential. I was aware of Spilka's critical analysis of existing research on religious development (1971), in which cited a series of major criticisms: "dubious validity," "too tuned to the inner voice of pure science," "lack of theoretical findings," and "inadequate attention to the relationship between personality and religion," among others.

I was equally aware of Clark's comment in his own summary: "The social scientist is not a theologian, and in concentrating only on his area of competence he may not be able to sense anything beyond it" (1971, 531). I was cognizant of Gordon Allport's comments two decades earlier, that "social scientists who study religions do not often enough think of the participants" and that the "religion of childhood may be of a very special order" (1950, 101). And, finally, as a kind of mandate for myself, I had read with concern the thoughtful words of Havighust and Keating concerning the neglect of interest in the religious views of the young:

> The feelings, aspirations and needs of the [child and] adolescent have a universality that transcends geography and time. . . . There is an amazing dearth of studies on the religious beliefs, interests, and concerns of American youth. If amount of research should be used as the criterion of importance, then the religious dimension would find a low place on the totem pole of values. (1971, 696)

With these comments echoing some of my own early intuitions, I chose my own path of inquiry with the children.

The Children

In deciding to interview forty children (twenty girls, twenty boys) of four different religious backgrounds, I felt that at least a relative diversity of young individuals would emerge. At the same time that diversity was important, the number of children needed to be manageable. Only with a reasonable collection of children could I enter into the introspective world of each child.

The four religions, each represented by ten children, were Catholicism, Judaism, Protestantism (Baptist), and Hinduism (American Ashram Group). These religions were selected because of their contrasting beliefs and because of the accessibility of their members. The first three were given preference over other alternatives because of their high prevalence and impact in

American culture. The last group, American-born children whose parents attend an ashram and identify with Hindu thought, was chosen particularly because its traditions presented a different world perspective. Moreover, this group of children could represent in minority status other small minority religious sects or sectarian viewpoints.

The children ranged in age from four to twelve years as of 1 January 1984. They were divided into three age groups (ages four to six; ages seven to nine; ages ten to twelve) for purposes of age socialization comparison. Thirteen children were placed in each of the two younger groups, while the ages of fourteen children indicated placement in the oldest group.

There was little question that older children could respond to the demands of the assessment tasks, even the play scenarios, provided they were presented in an official and tactful manner. Whether or not the youngest group of children, ages four to six, were appropriate for the study became a pivotal question. Would they be excessively inhibited by cognitive limitations? Would they be comfortable enough with me to provide original responses rather than parrotlike renditions? Would their attention spans be considerable enough to complete the interviews? From several pilot interviews I performed with children of this age group, I decided that these youngsters indeed had a contribution to offer and could provide a useful means of age comparison and perspective. Again the words of Havighurst and Keating were a source of confirmation:

A large proportion of the American population begins to construct systematic belief and disbelief systems about the universe in which they live, including the natures of physical and social reality and God, by about four to six years of age. (1971, 697)

These children were selected by their religious school teachers, representing the following four sites in Ann Arbor, Michigan: Saint Patrick's Catholic Church, the First Baptist Church, Hebrew Day School, and the Siddha Yoga Dham Ashram. First, I found a designated religious education leader who agreed to ask ten children and their parents to participate. I requested that the teachers choose a cross-section of children, those who apparently were less interested in religious training as well as those who actively participated. I also asked that they try to select equally among the age groups and equally between boys and girls in each group.

The teachers were told that my project was an investigation of religious development and that the children would be interviewed and asked to perform some creative tasks. If any parents elected not to participate, then other families were included on the particular list that I received. With any list that included more than ten families, I contacted the first ten.

With those families who agreed to participate, that is, both child and parents consented, it was first confirmed that the families formally identified with their respective religious groups. Like the teachers, the parents and children were told that the study concentrated on children's original religious views, that the interview process would take about two hours, and that the children would receive two small gifts for their participation (a Michigan banner and a set of drawing pencils).

The backgrounds of the parents were generally quite varied, according to their responses on a parental information questionnaire. Parents in each religious group and age group included lawyers, plumbers, and housewives. All could be described as "middle class," though they reflected quite a range of incomes. Some were single-career families (seventeen), while others were dual-career (twenty-three). Only two families, one in the Baptist group and one in the Hindu group, had divorced parents. In each case, the mothers had custody and the fathers lived in the vicinity. Ethnic representation was especially heterogeneous; in regard to racial representation, three black children (in each of the Catholic, Protestant, and Hindu groups) and two Asian-American children (in Catholic and Protestant groups) were included in the sample.

Since all the families resided in the Ann Arbor area and their permission was essential for participation, these considerations may have shaded our view of children and religion. I felt that any socializing effects of these concerns, however, would at least not be as pronounced as more directly influential variables like religion, age, or sex. In any event, children in highly different communities might on the surface have presented only slightly different deity representations. It is perhaps impossible to speculate concerning the effects of parental permission on the children's responses.

The Procedure

The logistics of interview scheduling were arranged in a follow-up telephone call. A suitable two-hour block of time was arranged, and I provided the families with directions to a convenient site on the campus of the University of Michigan. Once the family arrived, I spoke briefly with them as a group, acclimated the child to the new surroundings, received questions, and then presented the parents with a parent information questionnaire. Once the parents left, I began promptly with the child, first introducing them to the tape recorder and explaining that we would take breaks if they requested (all breaks were recorded).

All interviews were tape recorded on a small, unobtrusive cassette recorder. I was careful to explain to the children that everything they said was confidential and would only be released upon their permission. While some children expressed some reservation regarding their performance, every child agreed to be recorded and most seemed to enjoy the experience once the interview process began. As nine-year-old Carin, a Catholic child, noted, "It's kind of fun to get to talk into the recorder; it makes you feel kind of important."

Following the conclusion of the interview, after the letter writing, the children were asked to comment on "what the experience was like" and to discuss "what stood out" from our time together. I included this informal segment as a way of helping the children "debrief" and relax after their reflective experience. At the same time, the children provided important feedback for me on my interviewing manner and on the nature of the tasks. A typical response, put forth by seven-year-old Lauren, a Hindu child, was, "Well, the interview questions were kind of hard, but I think they're the kind of things that are good to think about. I thought the question about E.T. and God was funny."

The Interview

The interview process was divided into six main segments, each of which was designed to collect some particular aspect of the children's religious imagery. I wanted to be as comprehensive as possible but not inundate the children with so many tasks that their most vivid memory of the experience would be fatigue. While some tasks and questions were aimed at behavioral assessment, others were established for a more dynamic analysis. A few questions, particularly those toward the end of the questions and answers segment, were more experimental and exploratory, though some children proved quite revealing in their responses to these questions. The interview segments are summarized in the following sections.

Naming the Deity

At the outset of our meeting, it was essential to establish a common language with each child. I did not want to impose my terminology, yet some means of common discourse was needed. After several pilot interviews, I decided to negotiate with each child what the subject of our meeting would be about. I explained that while I was indeed interested in their ideas about the whole world, I wanted them to say what was most important in the world *for them*. Thus I decided to have the children begin with the most central aspect of the world as they saw it. I presented to each participant the following formula: "What word or words would you use to describe the most important thing in your beliefs?"

If the response to this inquiry seemed particularly difficult for an individual child, I probed lightly into his or her inner world until some capsule phrase emerged or, alternatively, until there seemed to be no such key phrase. The rest of the meeting concentrated on this phrase or word, the child's term for a deity.

Drawing the Deity

For those children who were more visual than verbal, a pictorial assessment of religious imagery was essential. Moreover, I knew that drawings have proved quite useful in clinical settings as a means of rapidly and graphically analyzing major conflictual themes (Machover 1949). I gave each child a sheet of construction paper and a dozen colored pencils and sent them off to draw as they wished.

Drawings have previously received some limited use in studies of religious affiliation. Harms, as early as 1944, had subjects draw pictures of the "Highest Being" because he felt that verbal questioning alone was misleading. Dennis (1966) emphasizes that drawings are excellent indications of the values and preferences of children's religious groups, as well as of the children's attitudes toward these groups. Klepsch and Logie, supporting these contentions, observe, "Of all the projective techniques, drawings dig deeper into the person, into his being" (1982, 36). In a study of religious imagery, projective drawing would seem a most advantageous tool.

Storytelling about the Deity

Once the children had completed their drawings, I asked them to tell a story about their work. Here I was particularly interested in how formal religion might emerge in relation to the original productions of the child. I gave them about five minutes to tell their story, and for most of the children, this was more than enough.

Among others, Elkind (1978) has pointed out that children's anecdotal information and stories can produce valuable insight into their religious constructions not so easily discovered by more highly structured means.

Playing the Deity

The next phase of the interview was perhaps the most novel and the most complicated. In order to make a behavioral assessment of religious imagery, I presented the children with a set of Flagg Family dolls, a flexible, lifelike group of five characters (mother, father, boy, girl, and baby), and asked them to "act as if they were the deity" in relation to this family. The children proceeded to act out and narrate three scenarios: (1) the entire family, (2) the parents alone, and (3) one child alone (the particular doll was chosen by the child-participant). While the child was acting out these scenes, I took notes and occasionally asked a probing question at the conclusion of each scenario.

Garvey (1977) has emphasized the imaginative richness of play and its role as a source of information about the child. Anna Freud has placed great clinical importance on children's play, as children seem to displace their internal struggles onto previously neutral play objects (Chrenka 1981). While play does not seem to have been used previously in studies of religious development, it seemed a most natural and appropriate mode of assessment, particularly as it provided a vehicle into the inner sanctum of the child.

Questions and Answers about the Deity

The interview proper was the most extensive part of the process and ordinarily lasted as long as the collective duration of the other tasks. In developing an interview strategy, I reviewed Piaget's "semiclinical method," in which structured questions are put forth but probing is determined by the unique responses of the child. Using a variant of this technique, I divided questions along the following categories suggested by pilot interviewing:

1. Description of the deity
2. Belief in the deity
3. Feelings about the deity
4. Communication/relationship with the deity
5. The deity and famous people

Elkind (1978) has been a most vocal proponent of the semiclinical method and its applicability to religious affiliation and prayer. Most religion researchers have adopted one interview technique or another, but there has been a recurrent tendency toward overstructuring and excessive directiveness, neither of which is conducive to the collection of spontaneous imagery.

Letter to the Deity

As a concluding collection technique, I asked the children to write a letter saying anything that they had left out or might like to say privately. I gave them about ten minutes to complete their correspondence. For younger children who requested it, I played the role of recorder in writing out their ideas verbatim. The major purposes of the letter were to search for any significant material which had not previously surfaced during the interview, and to gather some impression of what the interview process had been like for the child. Among others, Weisz (1980) supports the validity of thematic content analysis of children's letters to significant others.

The interview and tasks are presented in the Appendix.

The Analysis

The compiling and interpretation of the interviews called for accurate transcription and then many careful hours of thematic consideration. For the purposes of typed transcription, four assistants were hired, each of whom completed ten interviews. The transcribers were instructed to record everything that was said, to note parenthetically any detectable semiverbal utterances (e.g., sneezes, sighs, etc.), and then to write their own impressions at the conclusion of the transcription. A typical transcriber response read as follows: "Artie is a very bright, mature twelve-year-old whose ambivalence about the God figure is apparent. Yet it is hard for Artie to openly express his doubt and resentment." These brief inferences served as a helpful guide to me as well as an educational exercise for the transcribers, all of whom were undergraduate psychology majors.

Once I received a typed transcription, I reviewed each subsection (e.g., the letter) with its outstanding themes, commenting in the body of the text in order to highlight relevant examples. Once a child's protocol had been thoroughly analyzed and grouped with my own notes taken immediately following the interviews, I recorded all of the child's themes and relevant impressions on a card identifying the child by name, age, religion, and sex. Each child's responses were summarized in this fashion. When all such analysis was completed, I had forty cards which could be easily reshuffled in various ways for purposes of group comparison. Similarly, I kept the transcribed and analyzed protocols at hand for ready examples and further examination.

The Interviewer

It is most difficult to account for the possible impact I may have had on the interview process. Since I conducted all forty interviews myself, my influence in the most general of ways was likely similar for each child. Yet my initial conversations and certainly my probing, which was determined naturally by the unique responses and omissions of each child, were quite varied and specialized. At the level of emotional interaction, no two interviews were identical or even similar.

Thus high degrees of variability and flexibility on my part were essential. Moreover, a substantial investment and involvement on my part were required to help the children feel comfortable enough to open up, both with their feelings and with their ideas. Thus I occasionally allowed myself to travel on tangents with the children, to allow the interviews to proceed as the children desired. At the risk as well as for the benefit of being a participant, I surmised that such an approach provided the best opportunity for a glimpse of the natural perspectives of the child. I believe that the chapters which follow represent the best testament for the chosen exploratory tract.

3

Religious Themes

Dear God,
I saw Saint Patrick's Church last week
when we went to New York. You live in a
nice house.

Frank

The religions represented by the children reflect dispar-
ate world philosophies and suggest diverging socialization experiences, even as the children may share some
common historical characteristics. This chapter, as well
as the three that follow, offers a descriptive presentation of those motifs which distinguish children of the
particular religious groups in my investigation. I do not
speculate here in great detail as to how these differences came to be, leaving this to works of comparative
religion, past and present, to complete. My guiding
purpose with each section of the following chapters is
singular: to describe those themes which best distinguish the deity representations of a particular group of
children and which definitively set those children apart
from children of other religious groups.

The Jewish Children
Historical Orientation

The ten Jewish children placed decided emphasis on a
deity that occurs within the realm of human history,
though this God is not bound by history. Again and
again, the children stress historical context and repeat-

edly mention that a certain event occurred within a specific era. In keeping with this historical orientation, the Jewish children evidence an uncanny appreciation for history as a subject and, even more to the point, demonstrate a timeless propinquity to their historical ancestors.

These group trends were most vividly portrayed in the pictures and related discussion of nine-year-old Miriam, whose drawing appears below. In depicting Moses and his followers in the act of receiving the Ten Commandments, Miriam gives her audience a "you are there" sensation. She talks about Moses with a striking sense of familiarity, a knowing sense that made me wonder if he resided just around the corner. Here, God is not portrayed; God's more tangible and knowable representative, Moses, is depicted. Moses' role as God's "stand-in" also reflects the importance of human history in Miriam's inner world. Miriam is not alone among the Jewish children in openly displaying the importance of history. Among others, five-year-old Harold summarized the prevailing view when he surmised that "even more [a parenthetical introduction to emphasize his point], God is part of our history, the history of the Jewish people."

As is perhaps evident, such an investment in history carries along with it an orientation toward the past. This tendency was clearly more prevalent in the words of the Jewish children than in the responses of other children, and it sometimes seemed to cause the Jewish children internal conflict. Yet most of them conveyed a certain understanding that the past was useful as a means of living in the present. Thus, in drawings, stories, and play scenarios, they rely upon desert or water imagery, adopted from biblical accounts, as a metaphor for the bad times and good times in their everyday lives.

Their deity is not alone in a historical context. The

Drawing by nine-year-old Miriam

children also frequently allude to personal ancestors. While Catholic, Protestant, and Hindu children are essentially two-generational in their themes, the Jewish children are less constricted by time and immediate familiarity. Even in fictitious, spontaneous stories, typical references include "my great-grandfather," "Aaron, who I am a descendent of," and "my father's family in Europe." All of these ancestral characters seem to carry out highly individualized roles with God, sometimes occupying the role of a moral messenger between God and the living.

In trying to understand the Jewish orientation to history, possible effects of the Holocaust should not be overlooked. The loss of family, along with the obvious intrusion of history into family lineage, might well have heightened the children's awareness of history and ancestry; this acute awareness seems to find its way into the religious imagery of the children. Certainly, such identifications with culture and ancestry have been observed in those closest to the Holocaust a generation earlier, that is, the children of concentration camp survivors (Heller 1982).

Concerning the long-standing importance of history in Judaism, as well as its role in Jewish education, theologian and historian Emil Fackenheim writes, "The ancient Midrash affirms God's presence in history. Modern man on his part, sometimes seemed compelled to deny it" (1970, 78). Despite Fackenheim's contention, the Jewish children seem to demonstrate a belief in a relationship between God and history. Moreover, as Fackenheim does in fact later argue, the children seem to accept as a mandate that "bearing witness to other nations" is part and parcel of this historical understanding. Thus the theme of historical orientation nearly approaches a moral imperative among many of the Jewish children.

Jewish/Non-Jewish Gods

The Jewish children also evidence a kind of separatist notion of deities, frequently contrasting "their God" with the deity that the Gentile children talk about. Children of the other three religious groups do not evidence such a split, at least not in such a pronounced manner.

Miriam, our nine-year-old biblical artist, simply

states in justification of her deity conception, "I'm Jewish." She emphasizes this as a basic construct and pivotal point of differentiation. Eight-year-old Nellie, responding even more stoically and bluntly to my request that she name the deity, refers to "my God." In doing so, she is adamant about excluding others who do not share this God (including, in her assumptive world, me).

As these girls suggest, the Jewish children indicate a pervasive sense of "us" and "them" in their responses. "Us" serves to represent the Jewish world; "them" refers to the Christian world. The children seem hyperalert to their minority status and even seem to exaggerate religious differences. This appears particularly true for females, who according to Jewish law carry a special importance as bearers of future Jewish children and as gatekeepers of Jewish ritualistic practice. But the minority or separatist consciousness, as emerging in the deity conception, is even more complex. There is an element of "chosenness" in the children's responses, as they interact with a deity that has selected them for a special divine mission. The individual personalities of the children seem to determine what that mission may be, with examples ranging from six-year-old Greg's vendetta (to fight Israeli wars) to eleven-year-old David's mission (to help make peace in the world).

In *Basic Judaism* (1947), Milton Steinberg refers to this phenomenon as "Jews manifesting their yoke of chosenness," a separation from other nations based on their special status. In his classic sociological contribution, written some ten years later, Nathan Glazer explains how this special consciousness, among other factors, leads to a heightened sense of difference:

> Aside from their relatively small numbers, the Jews
> diverge in other respects from the major religious

groups in the United States. These divergences are
the result of the original character of their religion,
the particular history of the Jews before they
arrived in America, and the nature of American
society at the time of the American Jewish migra-
tions to this country. (1957, 3)

Relation of the Deity to Suffering

Children representing the Jewish religious group
clearly seem to be the descendants of the biblical Job.
They evidence frequent association of God with suffering and with questions related to suffering. Moreover, they present many recurrent themes of injury and
pain, resulting in increased doubt in or acceptance of
the deity. The ten children also convey a sincere empa-
thy for troubled persons, even when the distant troubles seem to have little personal relevance. Sometimes,
the children even seem to be lamenting the pain of the
world.

During introductions and her naming of the deity,
eight-year-old Nellie offered independently of any clear
precipitant, "There is a part of Jewish prayer, in the
Amidah [prayer book] which you say when someone is
sick or something." But why should Nellie so spontaneously make such a reference? I believe that, in part,
suffering imagery is unusually accessible to her and her
Jewish peers. At the same time, there is a certain
poignant plea and communication to me as her psychol-
ogist-interviewer. She unconsciously intrudes into the
dialogue some pain that she harbors, as well as a
concern about potential harm.

Some of the other children place their own unique
stamp on the suffering motif. In six-year-old Keith's
play scenarios, God cries as a young boy dies. Much as
the deity might try, it cannot save the drowning boy, a
child with whom Keith identifies. Six-year-old Harold

inadvertently weaves together the themes of pain and the Jewish/Gentile dichotomy. In a much less somber tone than Keith, Harold humorously quips, "It doesn't hurt to do a Christian sport and doesn't hurt a Christian to do a Hebrew sport." Apparently, Harold is sorting out his feeling toward the larger Christian world and any fears of injury that greater assimilation might engender. In Harold's words, one detects a growing sense of a more benign deity.

With most of the Jewish children, God is not depicted as a being who desires them to suffer. Usually, they ambivalently suggest, God maintains a purpose for suffering, helps them with suffering, or alleviates their suffering. Jewish children showed the largest religious group representation among those children who described a "therapist God"—a deity whose principle function was to help with troubles and problems. Also, a review of the children's references to suffering reveals a close relationship between suffering and guilt, a common focus of much psychotherapeutic work. At the same time, a long-standing Jewish cultural identification with suffering is also apparent.

The cultural origins of the suffering motif are most prominent in the later chapters of Isaiah in the Old Testament, where the Jews are purported to agree to suffer. They make this covenant with the Creator, the story goes, in exchange for the special privilege of serving him. While none of the Jewish children even approaches this extreme view, a cultural imprint still remains evident. Concerning more recent Jewish suffering, Richard Rubinstein speaks representatively for other Jewish historians in *After Auschwitz*:

> The Jewish community has experienced more monumental changes in the twentieth century than at any other time in its very long history. The uprooting involved in the emigration of millions of

Jews from eastern Europe to the United States and Canada, the death camps, and the rebirth of Israel each represent enormous alterations. Any one of these by itself would have been enough to create extraordinary problems in Jewish life; their occurrence in relatively rapid succession has created religious and cultural problems of unparalleled magnitude. (1976, 126)

In no way do the children display unparalleled problems or pain. However, their tendency to identify with pain is troublesome even to a naive outside observer.

The Catholic Children

God's Involvement in Marriage
and the Family

In comparison with their peers who are affiliated with other religious groups, Catholic children present a picture of a God who is intimately involved in family life. This deity is prominently and actively involved in family decisions and family tensions; it frequently helps to bring family members closer and helps them to stay together.

Dan, age 8, whose pictorial conception appears below, tells the accompanying story of "Jesus teaching to an ordinary person." According to Dan, the relationship of deity to person is the bond between teacher and student, or "other close relationships in the family." Not surprisingly, Dan's own relationship to his father has a similar quality. Later, in discussing the views of other family members, Dan mentions that his father often comes into his room at night to discuss the Bible, just as God enters into people's lives. In addition to this semideification of his father, Dan portrays a God image that is largely under the rubric of the family household.

Other Catholic children relate God and the family in

Drawing by eight-year-old Dan

a more indirect and usually less intrusive way. For example, divorce is a common theme for these children in play scenarios and the deity typically plays an interceding role, usually through communication with each of the parents. For several children, when the "parents alone" scenario is underway, tensions develop and God quietly intervenes, helping them to sort out their differences and reminding them of the Catholic Church's opposition to divorce.

Clearly, these interpersonal issues of marriage and divorce are somehow more central to the Catholic children than they are to other children, at least as far as the deity conception is concerned. While at the same time they manifest tremendous anxiety around a possible parental "break-up," a few also indicate an underlying wish for the forbidden separation to occur. While all children may bear a certain anxiety about the wish for a parental split, this anxiety seems exacerbated for the Catholic children as a result of their interpretation of Catholic practice. Consequently, God emerges in a "Pope-like" role, as the holy arbiter and as a symbol of family cohesion. For these Catholic children, the deity image sometimes serves the purpose of momentarily alleviating family-related fears and ensuring an intact family life.

In his well-known *The American Catholic*, Andrew Greeley also observes that family concerns represent a distinguishing motif in Catholic culture and constitute an enduring cultural trait:

> Family ties for American Catholics, then, are not only stronger for children and adolescents, they also persist into adult life. Catholics feel a greater obligation or need for, or a greater delight in, interacting with their parents and siblings than do Protestants and Jews. (1977, 209)

Greeley makes the point more globally and confidently than I find evidence for here, but this same inclination in my interviewees was clearly evident.

Concern with Guilt and Purity

Although it is a theme visible among some Jewish children and individual youngsters in the other two groups, a concern with guilt and purity is most endemic in the group of Catholic children. In their completion of tasks and interview responses, the Catholic partici-

pants manifest guilt in regard to three discernible
concerns: (1) sexuality and excitement, (2) anger, and (3)
what we might call "the existential human condition."
In dealing with budding sexual feelings, nine-year-
old Carin describes a male God who playfully leaves his
shower; then, as if undone by her guilt, Carin notes he
is "covered." Moved by guilt and anxiety, she removes a
young female character from the scene. In struggling
with troublesome angry feelings, nine-year-old Ted refers to some embittered friendships in his concluding
letter. Clearly, some residual guilt about his anger
needs to be absolved:

Dear God,
  God, please help me to like people that do bad
things to me and help me to do nothing to them.
Thank you.

Love,
Teddie

Last, eleven-year-old Laura displays her guilt concerning the existential human condition of poverty. In her
"child alone" scenario, her deity descends to the little
girl's playroom and firmly states, "Next time you have
your birthday you are to give the children of the poor a
toy or doll."
These guilt concerns of the Catholic children are both
explicitly and implicitly present in their protocols, re-
flecting some mixture of conscious and unconscious
guilt. Sometimes, the children seem to believe the guilt
is deserved and that the deity is legitimately bestowing
that guilt. At other times, the children seem to question
their guilt and thus frequently undergo a difficult cycle
of guilt and anger toward the deity.
The appearance of guilt is ordinarily followed in
responses by a concern with purity and by eradication
of the guilt, or by the fear of punishment, and by light
self-punitive measures (e.g., when Laura detracts from

her birthday by giving gifts to poor children). In these alternative scenarios, God is the one to whom the child is answerable; God is sometimes the source of punishment as well. In such forms, the deity approaches the God of the Catholic confessional, for it occupies the role of conscience in the child's inner world.

Belgum (1963) makes the intriguing point that guilt is a principal meeting point of psychology and religion, suggesting that this is particularly true of the Catholic religion. In his understanding, guilt is seen as a psychological turning away from the deity and from religious dogma. The guilty individual has temporarily "lost his identity as a child of God." However, for some of the Catholic children, their guilt seems less rational and easily explainable, perhaps a more complex interplay of religious and family dynamics.

Forgivingness

Among the Catholic children, the motif of forgivingness arises along with more negative feelings like anger or jealousy. This sense of forgivingness seems a learned response in keeping with the teachings of Jesus and Catholic doctrine. It may well be communicated through the atmosphere in Catholic families. The motif is characterized by a sense of understanding, acceptance, and tolerance of others. Forgivingness sometimes emerges in opposition to guilt or as a means of making amends for guilt and perceived sin. It is as if the child is saying, "To err is human, to forgive is divine."

Eleven-year-old Sean is one of the few children who expresses this theme of forgivingness quite openly. In answering the "God versus Jesus" question at the conclusion of the interview, Sean distinguishes between them through a particular function of Jesus: "God created Jesus so he could come down and forgive our sins." Other children, speaking in the spirit of everyday pragmatism, quietly associate forgivingness with deeds of the heart. This is echoed in the words of eleven-year-old Laura, in response to questions about God's "everyday activities":

People make things, like buildings, lightbulbs, electricity [Laura's father is an electrician], and Jesus loves them for this. But if they do something wrong, Jesus loves them anyway and tries to make things better.

For Laura, true forgivingness is demanded when an act is most difficult to forgive. In many of her responses, she suggests that for the Catholic children forgivingness involves reaching deeper into one's self in order to give.

On the subject of forgivingness, Hans Küng (1981) presents a widely held interpretation of Catholic doctrine. Küng emphasizes the need for people to learn to live with conflicts and errors at the same time that they attempt to resolve them. He also echoes the common view when he suggests that errors serve a function in reminding us of our essential humanness. Laura, too, would support this view, as indicated by her answer to the question about guilt feelings: "I feel guilty when I say something mean to my sister, but then I remember that people make mistakes—I realize I should not be harsh to either of us."

The Baptist Children
Nurturance Imagery

The Baptist children introduce a theme of nurturance, a motif in which God is associated with providing for mankind. While children from other groups occasionally make reference to such divine functions, they do not do so as frequently. Most often, nurturance imagery, sometimes called "oral imagery," appears among the Baptist children as a symbol of the deity or as a wish for increased nurturance from the deity and, symbolically, from the children's parents as well.

Nurturance often assumes a very literal meaning for the Baptist children in the form of references to food. This trend is humorously communicated by twelve-year-old Tom:

> Dear God,
>   How is it in heaven? How is it being the "Big Cheese"?
>
> Tom

Other children's expressions are more overt and serious than Tom's endearing letter. Ten-year-old Annette, for example, poignantly provides a set of play scenarios which focuses on God's attendance at a family dinner. Here, Annette forms her deity representation out of her desire for increased family nurturance. There also seems to be some subliminal association between the deity and Annette's mother, the provider of dinners, particularly in the way that Annette concludes the family scenario: "And God planned the family's dinner and saw that it was good."

Reviewing such quotes from the Baptist children reveals that their God figure is centered around these nurturance needs. The appearance of the nurturance theme may in part be due to a real-world pragmatism about worldly necessities. There also may be some common caretaking difficulties in Baptist family dynamics which result in the children's preoccupation. In any case, the children do seem to be struggling between receiving from the deity versus nurturing themselves.

In *The Baptizing Community* (1982), which encompasses Protestant groups in general, Theodore Eastman offers a possible theological basis for this nurturance motif. He notes that the act of baptism reflects a person's incorporation "into Christ" and into "the nurturance of the human family": "It is this incorporating or grafting aspect of baptism that nurtures young Christians so that they may grow strong in the faith and serve others in the world" (1982, 107). Even if Eastman is correct about the connection between symbolic religious imagery and individual personality, this does not discount the likely influences of the Baptist family as a socializing agent. Family members, after all, represent the interpreters of religious ideology.

Emotional Reserve

For the ten Baptist children, the deity appears as a somewhat reserved figure. Though God images do not necessarily appear as physically distant from the child, an emotional distance is evident between God and child.

For example, eight-year-old Dina recounts a story of Jesus' capture by Roman centurians with indifference and bland affect. Even her expression of "happy feelings" is unconvincing and belies deep emotional investment. For six-year-old Edith, God seems a highly involved and significant figure, particularly when he grants her desired gifts. Yet when asked about her feelings toward this deity, Edith grows cautious and tentatively utters "God is nice" in an uninspiring, staccato fashion. Both Dina and Edith seem to be holding back, circumspect about greater affective investment in their deity representations. It is not that they are uninterested or that their deities are insignificant to them, but that they seem fearful. They are concerned about how much to invest, perhaps a reflection of religious or interpersonal doubt and mistrust. They particularly avoid any visible expression of sentiment.

It is highly likely that family dynamics form the basis for this reserve. The Baptist children demonstrate a similar hesitance while discussing their family members, though their reluctance in this regard is less pronounced. Yet it may well be that the prevailing

affective tone of the Baptist families, or their relationship to emotional experience in general, transfers to the
children's conception of a deity.

But Protestant tradition and ideology may also be an
important factor. As theologian Martin Marty notes in
a discussion of comparative religion (1972), Christian
history emphasizes the cognitive dimensions of belief
rather than the emotional. The Baptist children,
through their imagery and responses, may reflect such
a cognitive emphasis on individual family members.

A God of Order and Organization

In the protocols of the Baptist children, the deity
emerges as one who represents order and organization,
giving structure to everyday life. While the deities of
other children may embody a unifying principle of the
universe, the Baptist conception presents an entity
that provides coherence in the child's own life. This
theme is especially recurrent among Baptist males,
perhaps as a result of the conventional masculine emphasis on order and structure. Thus the theme may well
reflect the complex interaction of two key socialization
factors: religion and sex.

Twelve-year-old Tom illustrates the sense of orderli-
ness and God's organizational functions. In responding
to the "involvement in birth" question, Tom contributes,
"Well, he decides if you are going to live or not, what sex
you're gonna be and what you're going to do or not. All
are planned ahead of time." Besides conveying a sense
of an orderly world, Tom evidently envisions life as pre-
determined and nonspontaneous. A sense of predesti-
nation is not so apparent in the words of twelve-year-old
Mark, though concern with order is no less potent. For
Mark, God provides order through "help in problem
solving" and "making sure that things happen in a way
that makes you learn from them." Moreover, Mark is
currently looking to God to provide "a different kind of

order," peace between his warring, quarrelsome parents.

Thus Baptist children tend to turn toward the deity to arrange, to structure, and ultimately to ameliorate their lives. For some of the children, this conception of the deity is associated with relinguishing a certain degree of freedom and personal choice. Males in particular struggle with the element of control and free will in response to the God of order and organization.

On the nature and role of order in the Protestant God conception, Marty writes:

> In Protestantism, believers are not called on to address the deity directly but to adhere to the order of things. . . . If Protestants have not been able to agree on many assertions, they have converged with remarkable concensus on the idea that men's strivings and sufferings are part of a movement in time, a movement with a beginning, a climax and an end. (1972, 187)

The Hindu Children
Community Unity

Above all, the Hindu children believe that the events of the ashram community as well as its members are interrelated. Despite some similar community orientation in the dogmas of the other religious groups, notably in Jewish culture, the children in these other groups do not demonstrate such a heightened awareness of community identity as does the Hindu group. While the ashram's minority status among places of worship must be a primary factor, the teachings of the ashram itself may well instill such a sense of unity.

Twelve-year-old Tamara, unusually articulate for her years, provides a good illustration of the community

unity theme. She responds to the "death of older person" question in the following manner:

It's all woven together, all these people's lives. So if one person is in a war, he might save twenty people .... If he had died before, all those twenty people would not have been saved. So everything is bound together in the community of persons.

Tamara's view seems to reflect a kind of "patchwork universe" in which individual threads are stitched together for the purpose of the community. There is an implicit indication in Tamara's words that the deity is weaving lives together.

Richard Mann, in *The Light of the Self* (1984), writes of the teachings of Swami Muktananda, who spent several years at the ashram that the children attend. Mann points out that this sense of community unity is stressed in education at the same time that the individual's consciousness is emphasized. In fact, the children's responses suggest a certain appreciation for this paradox. As seven-year-old Lauren mentioned, "I feel good about myself when I chant—but I like being part of something too."

Paradox: Greater Anthropomorphism/Less Anthropomorphism

There is a second paradox that the Hindu children articulate more explicitly. While the children describe a deity close enough to be a real person, they concurrently maintain that God is an abstract force or form of energy. This paradox seems to exist in the children's responses regardless of their age.

Anthropomorphism is particularly indicated in the protocols of four children, two of each sex, who chose to respond to their tasks and questions in terms of "Baba," a human sage or guru they had known and believed to be endowed with the spirit of the deity (in three cases, this was Swami Muktananda). As five-year-old Erin explained, "God and Baba are almost the same... God is sort of inside Baba." Erin's qualifier, that "God is inside Baba," speaks to the conception of the deity as a process or force rather than as a person alone. Tamara, seven years the senior of Erin, refines this sense of a more abstract God:

> I think it is supposed to be a force. God is not so much a person. He's in so many people, and he's everywhere. He's everywhere and everything.

In Tamara's expansive account, she strongly hints that she has been taught this understanding, though it is not crystal clear to her.

This twin view, the notion of both a tangible and intangible deity, makes the children's God immediate and personally available at the same time it makes the deity mysterious. But the sense of mystery that the Hindu children intimate is not one of fear and bizarreness. The deity is an enigma and largely associated with anticipation and wonder, along with confusion. In each case, this conception seems to cultivate a growing spiritual curiosity in the children. Ultimately, the youngsters must try to make sense of the intriguing duality.

The interviews reflect the essential paradox in Hindu thought. According to the Hindu tradition, the world is made up of *shiva*, a supreme reality that is formless, unknowable, and transcendent. Yet the world is also comprised of *shakhti*, the simultaneous presence of this reality as it manifests itself as conscious energy (Mann 1984). In terms of the more direct socialization of these children, it should be remembered that the Baba Muktananda was for some of them an important part of their early education. One of his principal tenets, in keeping with the theme of anthropomorphism/nonanthropomorphism, might be stated as follows: If one wishes to experience more fully the latent or sacred world, one should enter into close contact with another person in whom the sense of the sacred dominates awareness (Mann 1984).

Intense Devotion

The Hindu children display an unusual zeal concerning their religious beliefs. Their responses are infused with emotional investment, yet they communicate in a reasonably lighthearted and nonevangelical manner.

Their play scenarios include numerous episodes of meditation or concentrated attention that do not emerge in the scripts of other children. This concentration is emotional in nature and influences the Hindu children's responses to interview questions as well. In reaction to the birth question, Tamara presents an interesting perspective on an unalterable relationship between deity and individual:

> I think even if the parents are not very religious and they don't believe in God, I think the child is still with God . . . that God still blesses the child and the child will still be dedicated to God.

What is most striking about Tamara's response is the intensity of investment that comes across, an intensity that appears to be tied to a desired independence.

Images of devotion are a cornerstone of Hindu thinking as well as of American adaptations of Hindu thought. This sense of dedication or investment, in its most reverent form, is sometimes called *darshan*—a certain experience of magical involvement in encountering the sacred (Mann 1984).

Epilogue: Religious Themes

The religious groups and their small standard-bearers present a most interesting, frequently loveable, and sometimes poignant parade of themes. Each group, through ideology, practice, and family dynamics, offers a strong socialization influence that begins to account for the God images of the children. Yet formal religion, however pronounced its impact, is but one major socialization factor. While formal religion clearly influences the individual, it most often does so through the filter of more immediate developmental and social factors. In pursuit of these concerns, I now move to a factor that has received the greatest attention in the psychological literature on children's religious differences: the age of the child.

4

Age Themes

Dear God,
  Do good people have to die young? I heard
my mommy say that. I am not always good.
                    Yours truly,
                    Barbara

Age is likely to play a significant role in the formation of a God representation, much as it does in the formation of parent or self-representations. In fact, most literature on religious development focuses on age differences. Contributors to this literature are inclined to downplay the maturity of children's conceptions even as they focus on the significance of childhood images. With the themes that unfold in this chapter, I have tried to refrain from assuming that the children's representations will be severely limited by age. The summaries that follow speak for themselves, just as the forty children do for their respective age groups.

The Four- to Six-year-old Children
Lack of Knowledge

The first age-related theme is the more readily apparent, and yet its nuances require explanation. The youngest group often displays a clear absence of information concerning established religion and the sociology of religion. For example, five-year-old Harold has little awareness of figures like God, Moses, or Gandhi. Instead, he focuses throughout on the few symbols he is familar with, using terms such as "temple," "Christians," and "Jews." Concerning God's relationship with "famous figures," Harold's only response, constructed to convince us that he is truly an astute observer of the world, is, "I don't know about them . . . [after some thought] But I do recognize the names."

The four- to six-year-old children do demonstrate greater recognition of standard religious concepts than recall of these items. Their awareness is selective: ideas of high salience, like those surrounding religious group identity, are quite accessible. This trend seems highly socialized at such an early age. Most of the children, in responding to the "learn about religion" item, mention only their parents and are quite vocal about their parents' heavy involvement in teaching them.

Sometimes, perhaps in trying to compensate for their level of knowledge, these young children are prone to distort religious facts. They demonstrate episodic confusion concerning religious categories as well as a Pollyannaish approach to these categories. The bases for these distortions seems to be misinterpretations of parental messages, and to a lesser extent, age-related cognitive limitations. Six-year-old Gerard presents a typical kind of confusion in his "God and Jesus" response: "Well, I know Jesus was a president and God is not . . . sort of like David was a king and God is not . . . like you're a David. Does that make you a king?"

In *A Sympathetic Understanding of the Child* (1978), David Elkind argues that cognitive limitations in fact thoroughly shape small children's responses. From the forty children in the current study, cognitive limits do play a role in information omissions and distortions, but interpersonal factors and religious educational experiences also seem significant.

Generalized Playfulness and Gaiety

The small children tend to maintain a positive and soft-mannered sense of a deity, frequently associating

God with play and fun. God is linked to simple, mundane pleasures and is generally permissive of the child's reveries. Four-year-old Marcie tells us about God's home: "God lives in a big castle, like our church; God also probably has a choir, and Christmas parties too!" Similarly, six-year-old Edith, a sports-oriented child with Aspen apparently in her future, says of her "love feelings": "I feel a lot toward God because he makes life happy and he lets you do fun things like skiing and stuff." Meanwhile, the more serious Barbie, age four, observes that God is with her when she makes drawings of flowers, which is something she enjoys a lot. Thus, with all three children, the deity is highly related to pleasure, to fantasies, and to simple aspirations.

Such benign imagery of small children is too often labeled "simplistic." But there is no reason to assume that they have less of an idea of truth than conceptions of the deity which are more fully elaborated. There is something strikingly natural about the gay manner of these children, at the same time that developmental and socialization changes are also apparent.

Sometimes the small children's playfulness is manifested in the spontaneous appearance of familiar characters to represent the deity. Even with more formal religious imagery, the reasonably happy four- to six-year-old seems to find a colorful, even silver lining. The best example comes from outside of my forty interviewees, from a woman who was gracious enough to share her six-year-old grandson's drawing with me. The youngster, a Catholic child, had been instructed in Sunday school to draw Jesus on the cross. His humorous drawing, which appears below, suggests that this six-year-old found the vision of a man on a cross much too negative. Clearly, something happier and less ominous was in order. Enter Bugs Bunny!

In an interesting book relevant to these issues (1967), Hugo Rahner discusses the shared elements of play and religion. Rahner draws from the writings of classical

Bugs's Easter

antiquity and the early Church. He emphasizes the Platonic elevation of play to the highest regions of the spirit. Certainly, the potential for high excitement in response to a deity of play is readily visible in our youngest group of children.

God Revolves around the Self

The four- to six-year-old children display a definite self-focus, in keeping with their developmental narcissism and the substantial attention that they probably receive from their parents. This self-focus profoundly influences God representations, as the various deities perform functions for the child and concentrate largely on the child's welfare. When asked about evidence for God's existence, confident Aaron, age five, replies, "God made me," indicating that this alone was sufficient proof. In like manner, seven-year-old Jeri believes in God because she gets presents and because God gives to her.

The standard psychoanalytic view of such a self-focus seems to explain the children's reactions adequately. In struggling with early narcissism, children of this age may be quite "event centered" in their experiences and in their explanations of experience. "I know because I experience" is the prevailing view, a perspective molded by developmental needs and early socialization and subject to change based on continuing socialization.

Duality of the Deity (Splitting)

In keeping with other developmental and socialization markers, these fledgling theologians indicate that a certain duality in the universe must be addressed. They portray a deity that is sometimes good and sometimes not, and occasionally one that is a mixed or ambivalent character. According to six-year-old Gerard, "Sometimes I feel that God is real nice, then sometimes I feel like God is bad." Five-year-old Aaron, precociously poetic, expresses a similar sentiment in metaphoric displacement. In his story, Aaron provides his own rendition of the Noah's Ark plot: "And God sends out two different kinds of birds to find dry land. One is a raven and one is a bluebird, and they're as different as the world is."

Apparently, the children are trying to comprehend the mixed nature of things in the world. They speak of their relationship to sunshine and rain as well as their relation to parental figures. For many of the children, it is easier to take good and bad feelings one at a time, to split their experiences into a "good God" or "bad God," or a quixotic God, neither wholly good or bad. For those children who find ambivalence particularly difficult and painful, displaced or metaphoric expression is especially prevalent. This unfortunate trend is no more true for any child than Aaron. In other responses, Aaron indicates an unusually embittered and intensely ambivalent relationship with his mother.

In *The Birth of the Living God* (1979), Rizzuto speculates that the splitting of the God concept speaks to an underlying division of parental representations. In other words, the child's internal parent images, good and bad, are projected onto the God concept.

The children's interest in both sides of life is not particularly surprising given the observations of Jean Piaget. In *The Child's Conception of the World* (1969), Piaget notes this concern with duality, and a simple curiosity about life and death, among five- and six-year-old children. Fowler (1981) offers a confirming observation concerning this special age group and its curiosities, relating their responses to their often divided feelings toward primary caretakers.

The Seven- to Nine-year-old Children
Increasing Knowledge and Curiosity

In contrast to their younger counterparts, the middle group of children demonstrate an increasing awareness of religious practices and figures, as well as a greater curiosity about formal conceptions of a deity.

These group trends are readily apparent in the ten children's responses to the "questions" and "changes" items in the section of the interview about communication with the deity. Nine-year-old Arthur asks God, "What's the future gonna be like?" Eight-year-old Nellie whimsically inquires, "Where is the Garden of Eden?" And nine-year-old Ted, the Art Buchwald of his generation, challenges, "Why does spinach have to taste like it does?"

For these inquisitors, their growing awareness and searching is intimately tied to their individual struggles and worries. Arthur is concerned about the future because of his parent's pending divorce. Nellie yearns for the Garden of Eden, a symbol of an earlier time when her life seemed more halcyon. Finally, Ted humorously demonstrates that personal concerns need not always be serious but may be as mundane as that dreadful vegetable. While these children's cognitive capacities may be developmentally affected, it seems that the particular form that their awareness and curiosity takes depends on their own individual socialization experiences. Elkind (1978) concludes from a series of studies on religious identity and prayer that such questions are neither entirely learned nor essentially innate. It is clear, however, that these questions are indeed triggered by life experiences.

It is precisely these types of questions that the talented children's writer, Judy Blume, concentrates upon in books like *Are You There, God? It's Me, Margaret* (1970). In this enchanting story, a young girl asks if God is listening and then repeatedly asks God for permission, a sanction to perform such everyday activities as a religious project. Blume is quite effective at bringing Margaret's developmental uncertainties and mixed socialization messages to the surface. As readers, we are left considering how difficult it is for a child to find his or her way, whether in terms of religious belief or self-conception. And often, Blume would have us believe, the two are inseparable.

A Deity Who Grants "Specialness"

The seven- to nine-year-old children express a tremendous desire to feel special and be viewed as special in the eyes of the deity. The yearning for self-importance goes far beyond a need to be loved; the child wants appreciation above and beyond others.

The best example of such desire is provided by nine-year-old Carin in her story:

> Once upon a time in Heaven . . . God woke up from his nap. It was his birthday. But nobody knew it was his birthday but one angel . . . And this angel rounds up all these other angels, and when he gets out of the shower, they have a surprise party for him.

As we shall later discuss, Carin identifies highly with this special angel. The craving for specialness is quite evident, even in Carin's description of the angel. Unlike the younger children, whose stories revolve more around themselves, Carin places the deity in a central position and tries to assume a royal place alongside this God. However, she leaves us with a sense that she is merely part of the group of angels, suggesting that her specialness is more wished for than real at present.

A major reason for the concern with specialness among the seven- to nine-year-old children is the continuing arrival of younger siblings, who represent to the older child the successors to parental attention. No longer is the older child the focus of the family. Gone are the days when family members stood around watching the child's every move. In their deity conceptions, the older children may try to resurrect their lost specialness with God, rather than with parents.

In regard to the inner struggle with specialness, theologian Wilfred Cantwell Smith speaks about adults in a way that may apply to our children as well: "Where only angels tread, he would be a fool to rush in, though perhaps the wise may preserve their dignity if, aware of their presumption, they enter cautiously" (1962, 154).

Aloneness and Nonaloneness

The middle group seem more aware of themselves as independent actors. As a result, they frequently ponder whether they are alone or not in relation to a deity. The children confront a difficult dilemma: it seems that they are alone more of the time than before and yet belief in a deity dictates that they are not alone. For some, loneliness is inescapable, while for others the opportunity for self-discovery and growth prevails.

In play scenarios, aloneness is a common motif. In the "child alone" section, eight-year-old Dan reports: "The little boy doll is lost in the store. He can't find his mother. He walks around and tries to find her. He needs God's help." Nine-year-old Ted related a similar script in his family scenario: "The child is alone because he's going to go away. His family has a lot of problems, so he's going to have to go to a foster home. God makes sure that he has food and a stable home."

As such examples suggest, the relationship between the child and the deity is heavily shaped by the child's current relation to family. Loneliness seems to creep in as the child realizes that the family will not always act as a protective shield against the vast unknown of living. Yet loneliness also develops within the family as family members fail to respond to the child's needs. In some cases, the child will cling to the family, as occurs in several of the children's play vignettes. In other cases, as with Dan and Ted, the child searches in his or her own awareness for a deity or new family that will rectify the situation.

Once again, Judy Blume nicely captures the tenor of this age group when her main character, Margaret, asks, "Why God . . . Why do I only feel you when I'm alone?" From the psychoanalytic point of view, Ana-Maria Rizzuto (1979) convincingly argues that some of the God imagery of this age period stems from an attempt to master the oedipal situation. According to Rizzuto, the child at seven is no longer allowed open access to the parental bedroom. The child experiences intensely this relegation to the role of observer outside of the parental dyad. Along with loneliness, a kind of inner searching and perhaps an external move toward siblings and peers take place. Rizzuto implies that the resulting God image is forged out of this interpersonal vacuum, the product of the child's predicament. Yet the possibility of an actual encounter between child and deity must also be considered, particularly as the child begins to struggle and question previous socialized beliefs.

Association of Deity with Sleep and Dreams

The seven- to nine-year-olds demonstrate a fantasy-linked, ethereal conception of a deity. They frequently suggest that sleep and dreams are a common meeting place between God and man. In keeping with this belief, God appears as a spiritlike image without much structure or definition.

Seven-year-old Hallie offers an exemplary illustration of these conceptions in her "child alone" scenario:

> Well, there once was a little girl. She was born but
> she didn't know who had her, and she walked and
> walked and walked . . . And then sat down, and
> said, "I'm going to sleep." And she sat down under
> a tree and went to sleep. In the night, she was
> visited by the spirit of God. Then in the morning,
> she awakens and sees a whole house set up for her.
> And she said, "Thank you, God." And there were

people for her to play with too, and they became her brothers and sisters.

The loneliness theme is right at the surface of Hallie's scenario but so is the sense of a divine spirit. While for some children the deity is musical as it emerges, Hallie's spirit comes quietly in the middle of the night. While for some children the deity appears through dreams, Hallie's deity arrives while she is sleeping but does not itself enter into her sleeping world. It does seem that Hallie's God develops in relation to her pain and aloneness, just as sleep and dreams may be a welcome respite from difficult developmental struggles. Ultimately, the deity performs the same kind of wish-fulfilling fuction that often occurs in dreams—Hallie is provided with a new home and friends for her enjoyment. Thus, in the tranquil and safe confines of sleep, Hallie meets her deity and her life is magically changed.

The relationship between sleep, dreams, and spirituality has been mapped extensively by Carl Jung. In *Psychology and Religion* (1938), Jung maintains that "dreams really speak of religion" and represent a central means of spiritual communication. This theme is even more common in classical and biblical literatures. In Greek plays and histories, dreams and oracles invariably convey to man the wishes and predilections of the gods. From the tragedies of Aeschylus to the comedies of Aristophanes, dreams are an accepted or even preferred form of spiritual expression (Ferguson 1980). Old Testament allusions to dreams and sleep are also common, perhaps culminating in the story of Joseph, the interpreter of dreams. Both the classical and the biblical conceptions suggest that dreams have prophetic importance and help people to work through everyday events. Both of these functions are also cited by the children in their stories and scenarios.

The Ten- to Twelve-year-old Children
*Definitive Knowledge versus Uncertainty
and Doubt*

The oldest group of children display the greatest knowledge of formal religion and religious imagery. At times, these children indicate a stronger conviction than others in their concepts and figures, yet their sense of doubt and hesitance is also more potent and pervasive.

This episodic but ardent belief in newly acquired knowledge emerges in various parts of the children's protocols. Twelve-year-old Mark says of his "love feelings":

> When I'm in Church, I feel like I'm sort of part of God. I'm helping people and doing things right. I'm doing things like Jesus did, but I'm doing what I want too.

Yet, Mark expresses doubt with great concern as well. On the subject of doubt, he volunteers:

> When I broke my arm—I've broken my arm four times—I wondered if He wanted me to break my arm. Was I having too much joy or something like that? Sometimes it makes me wonder.

Mark's conflict between faith and doubt seems to overlap with a continuing battle between fate versus self-control, a tension that is shared by many members of his age group. Aggressive feelings toward the deity, or toward a deity with parental overtones, is also implicit here as Mark voices his displeasure. As much as Mark is developing a firmer sense of himself, he shows an increasing awareness of life's uncertainty.

Rizzuto (1979) refers to the struggles of this age group as a kind of combat—a battle between the God of religion and the God of the child. The battle is begun by the children's budding recognition that this formal God does not always work so well, as Mark implies. As a consequence of this awareness, the child will begin to do much reshaping and rethinking as adolescence ensues. Philosophically, Kierkegaard's distinction between faith and doubt is a good way to describe what the older children express. The nature of these evolving and transitional years demands that both faith and doubt be rather temporary. Thus we might consider that the conceptions of the ten- to twelve-year-olds are characterized by the following two statements from Kierkegaard (1946, 208):

"I can't see him, but I can imagine and I believe."
"I can't see him because there is nothing to be seen."

It is the difficult circumstance of the child that he or she seems to oscillate greatly between these two alternatives.

Concern with Injury or Pain

The oldest group of children, perhaps feeling less protected by parents, seem to fear injury or pain in various forms. Either the deity is the deliverer of injury or the deity is expected to deliver the child from pain. Unlike the group of Jewish children, who identify with suffering in a more or less enduring way, the ten- to twelve-year-olds do not identify with long-term suffering but fear more transient pain and obstacles.

Current wounds or the potential for injury stand out in most of the interviews with these children. For example, in the "child alone" scenario, ten-year-old Scott tells of a little boy who steps on a nail, a true-life saga with only the names changed to protect the storyteller and his parents. When asked about doubt, twelve-year-old Tamara informs us of her growing skepticism and resentment after she received third-degree burns. For some of the children, the expression of injury occurs through displacement. Twelve-year-old Tom, for example, offers a poignant family scenario about a broken vase and a little boy who is blamed for the damage to this family heirloom.

The injury motif suggests that children of this age group have moved further away from self-centeredness. They seem quite aware of the reality that not all things are tailored for their needs and, moreover, that pain and injury are real. In addition, they are beginning to view their family with something of an observer's eye, and the view is not always idyllic. Pain expressed through displacement or metaphor often acts as a symbol for family difficulties or emotional injury. At the same time, in keeping with a developing relationship to the media, the children understand that there is much injury and unhappiness in the world.

Where a deity fits into this picture is not at all clear to the children. They frequently begin to attempt explanations, usually painting a portrait of a savior God, but eventually their uncertainty is transparent. They are left asking two elemental questions: (1) What is God's role in suffering? (2) Why does God let one feel pain? The children were honest and wise enough to acknowledge that they really did not have answers to these questions. They were also thoughtful and empathetic enough not to ask me directly.

Writing on this topic in *When Children Ask about God* (1971), Rabbi Harold Kushner maintains that formal religious imagery is too often associated with injury and suffering and this can precipitate tremendous fear in children. While Kushner emphasizes the socialization influence of the religious dogma here, we might speculate that such socialization images interact with difficult developmental concerns to shape the older child's God representation.

However, in *Does God Exist* (1981), Hans Küng offers a contrasting interpretation. Küng believes that suffering, being part of the reality of life itself, can often bring the adult or the child closer to God. Succinctly, his view is that "the mystery of the Incomprehensible in its goodness also encompasses the wretchedness of our suffering" (1981, 423). In this way, Küng attempts to provide some answer to the kind of questions that spontaneously emerge from the children.

Concern with God's Scope

The ten- to twelve-year-old children evidence curiosity about the purview of the deity, an interest in whether this deity has any limitations at all. With this theme, the children try to respond to the ambiguity and the enigma of popular and formal representations of God.

In considering the "everyday activities" question, twelve-year-old Gerald offers, "God touches every aspect of my life, from homework to prayer. At least, I think he does." Twelve-year-old Tom comments, "God helps you no matter what. I believe he's there with you all of the time." Last, ten-year-old Irma informs us more directly, "I'm not clear what God can't do."

The interest in the deity's limitations, or absence of limits, seems to reflect the children's concern about their own limitations. Most often, as Gerald and Tom in particular illustrate, God performs and compensates for many of the things that are clearly outside of the child's repertoire. As they grow, the children are beginning to learn what they cannot do, and this becomes one of the most difficult ongoing lessons of childhood. In addition to the influence of formal religion, which may draw a picture of an unlimited and uncategorizable God, the children themselves construct their representations out of their developmental struggles. Ultimately, the children are realizing that they cannot have an impact on all things.

Rizzuto (1979) maintains that every phase of an identity crisis, as she calls it, may bring with it a reevaluation or reaffirmation of the religious conception. While it is not certain that this occurs at every developmental point, it does seem to appear in these ten- to twelve-year-old children.

Concern with Afterlife

Compared to the children in the other age groups, these older children spontaneously make more frequent references to life after death and express curiosity about the nature of existence.

There is substantial variety and individual difference in what the children have to say about afterlife, however. Some children, like twelve-year-old Mark, imagine an afterlife that is very active. In the course of answering the "older person's death" question, twelve-year-old Tamara offers,

Everyone must make their own special destiny once life has passed. After you die, you still make your own choices and your life after death depends a lot on what your life before was like. Mostly, it depends on you.

Other children present a picture of a more tranquil afterlife, an existence that differs markedly from everyday life. Lorraine, age twelve, provides a good example in the "everyday activities" section of her interview:

But God is involved with people in a different way. God helps people to make a change to a different place after they die. I think heaven is real peaceful. I think life is a search for this peace.

This dichotomy among the children perhaps reflects what different children would like as they leave childhood. The afterlife conception, naturally emerging in these older children, seems to reflect the move toward adolescence and young adulthood. Some children seem to crave greater independence and an active life style. Others, perhaps influenced by family tensions, anticipate life will be more peaceful as they begin to leave the family. What both types of children have in common is that afterlife represents an improvement, either a return to an earlier blissful state or a move toward a new and happier existence.

In *Life after Life* (1976), Raymond Moody suggests that everyone carries preconceptions about afterlife and that specific life events can cause these preconceptions to surface. Whether or not developmental struggles or socialization experiences can have such an effect is arguable, though the children seem to use the concept of afterlife to convey some of their thoughts concerning their more immediate future and development.

Epilogue: Age Themes

The age themes of the forty children reflect a mixture of developmentally set and socially triggered influences. These multiple influences overlap deity representations with a number of transitional motifs, each of which conveys important information about the children's inner struggles.

The youngest group of children, ages four to six, illustrate a largely single-minded conception of a deity, a being who acts and appears in a quite literal rather than abstract sense. To cope with negative feelings, these children seem to split the deity into competing forces or figures. While the deity may be important to the child, this level of significance does not always transfer into informed information about the deity's activities.

The middle group, children from ages seven to nine, demonstrate greater curiosity about the deity and its role in human life. Deity conceptions are markedly interpersonal, with parental attention or its absence an underlying concern. The deity takes on a mystical or even mysterious aura as it becomes associated with the child's nocturnal activities; it is the deity of sleeping and dreaming. Also, these children display increasingly complex and abstract notions of God and spirituality.

The oldest group, ages ten to twelve, present the most abstract and highly developed conception of God. There is considerable religious doubt in these children, doubt that is both acknowledged and strongly implied. They are fairly cognizant of established religious views, though owing to their generalized doubt, they are not at all certain about these views. Increasingly, deity imagery is associated with independence strivings and a budding awareness of possible limitations. The children also express an expectancy about pending change and a curiosity about the unknown that, when connected to the deity, carries something of the feeling of an adolescence soon to be lived.

5

Gender Themes

Dear God,
Are boys better than girls? I know you are
one (a boy), but try to be fair.
Sylvia

In recent years, it has become popular at public meetings to introduce semihumorously the idea that God may be "of the feminine persuasion." Such proclamations are usually invoked in the spirit of equal rights, to counter what is considered a largely male-oriented conception of a deity. Such contemporary statements of belief or antibelief, which assume a God that is sexual in an anthropomorphic sense, raises the question of sexuality in the children's conceptions. Do children ages four to twelve in fact perceive God in this way? And also, how do boys and girls, these future men and women, differ in their thematic representations? I thought it might be highly informative and interesting to explore this important and controversial socialization influence.

The Male Children
A Rational Deity

The twenty boys in the study describe a deity with a heavily rational and pragmatic orientation to human life and to the world at large. These boys emphasize a thinking and knowledgeable God, a deity that demonstrates omniscience and guides individuals in relatively comprehensible and predictable ways. A great deal of the deity's power is derived through this acumen.

Lenny, age ten, illustrates the importance of knowledge and rationality when he responds to the "everyday activities" question: "God understands what people think." Yet apparently Lenny's God is not only an understanding God, but a God that also acts in a rational manner. Later, he provides an example of how God intervenes in human affairs:

> If you need 25 cents, he makes sure you get it. But he is reasonable. You don't get it in a bad way, like stealing or something. But he'll make sure you deserve it, and you get it in time for good things . . . like bubble gum. . . . That's the way the world is.

Apparently, Lenny's deity is not only reasonable but sensitive enough to get desired treats to a child on time.

For many of the male children, God's rationality is tied to the governing of science. For these youngsters, the extraterrestrial Being is unequivocally a "God of Science." Scott, also ten years old, creatively explains where God lives:

> It's a planet, like you need special glasses to see it. First, you need to get past the sun and then you have to get past the planets, and then you have to have enough power to get out of the galaxy. . . . And then, and only then, you might find it.

Scott's elusive but astronomy-oriented God resembles the conceptions of several other youngsters. Five-year-old Keith is a good representative of the smaller boys. When asked to name the deity at the outset of the interview, Keith informed me that he would like to talk about "God" and about "space." I then became the captive audience of this miniature Carl Sagan. It certainly seems that Scott, Keith, and the others, with their spontaneous references to time, space, and energy, are very conscious of a technological and rational age. This consciousness pervades their deity imagery.

In *Magic, Science, and Religion* (1955), anthropologist Bronislaw Malinowski goes to great lengths to distinguish between the sacred/religious realm and the profane/rational realm. Yet my male interviewees show no such division. For these selected children, rationality and religion seem to reside in their responses in a state of peaceful coexistence. If anything, religion and rationality are highly integrated, while the possibility of a more feeling-oriented approach to the sacred is cast aside. Perhaps these children demonstrate what William James called "a certain blindness" (Vanden Burg 1981), a rationalization of emotional interest in the spiritual, rooted in the implication that such emotionality is either nonexistent or false.

More specifically in regard to sex differences, it comes as little surprise that the boys present such a rational conception. For the most part, Western society still demands this of males, renders it functional for them, and rewards them greatly for accomplishment in rational endeavors. It seems that even today boys are far more concerned with the affairs of the state and the rational order of things than, for example, the affective affairs of the family (McMillan 1982). Thus this age-old socialization phenomenon finds its way into conceptions of God, God's practices, and God's way of being.

Active Orientation

The male children depict a deity thoroughly active in the life of man; this deity asserts itself on all planes in order to achieve its desired ends. Rather than setting things in motion and then assuming a place as a bystander, God is incessantly working toward some instrumental goal. It is in this way that God extends himself to man.

Several children are quite emphatic in their contention that God participates actively in events. Six-year-old Gerard, in responding to the "everyday activities" inquiry, reveals a God who not only watches over Gerard's sports endeavors but actually engages in vigorous activities "like swimming" himself. The paternal etchings in Gerard's response are mirrored by those in the answers of ten-year-old Lenny, who portrays a philanthropic deity in his "child alone" scenario. In Lenny's rendition, God picks up a man who trips over a tree and intercedes in the man's difficulties, difficulties such as a long-standing dispute with the man's brother.

With this active, "events" orientation, a fatherlike figure emerges within the children's imagery. The children insist that the figure be active, and they even intimate an antagonism toward any hint of passivity. "Taking charge" is the sine qua non of the figure. It is not clear, however, whether Gerard and Lenny create this image out of identification with their fathers or out of a wish to improve on their fathers' manner.

The essential goals of the deity in this active regard are twofold: (1) to communicate with the child; (2) to improve the child's life through actions. As Lenny says, "God communicates as if he is talking long distance . . . with what he does." Here Lenny makes us wonder if he desires even greater closeness with an apparently benign father, father image, or deity. It is clear that he trusts this representation and believes that God works for his betterment. Along with those of Gerard and the other male children, Lenny's God conception reflects "a man of actions" and these actions seem to speak louder than words alone.

Such an emphasis on activity is a very typical component of male socialization. Sigmund Freud spoke of such a relationship between masculinity and activity throughout his works:

In every field of psychic life a male child tends to

react actively to impressions received passively. In love relations there is the same opposition between "active" and "passive": men love and women let themselves be loved. (1933, 106)

While Freud intends his view to speak for an innate biological inclination as well as a historical socialization phenomenon, it is this second interest that is most to the point for our discussion. A socialization perspective is echoed in some of the growing contemporary literature on conceptions of masculinity. Concerning the socialization of masculinity, and by implication the male deity representations, Karl Bednarik writes in *The Male in Crisis* (1970) of this intractable active orientation. Bednarik argues that the two principal avenues for male self-fulfillment have been active— fighting and working—and that this circumscription of fulfilling investment is psychologically costly and no longer tenable.

The Great Distance of the Deity

On the whole, the boys' representations indicate that the deity is relatively or at least episodically distant. While for a few boys God is geographically distant, for nearly all of them, the deity is emotionally distant even as God is actively involved in the child's life.

Among others, six-year-old Gary describes a deity who lives in the desert, away from people, while he does things to help them. Twelve-year-old Tom reports that his deity is "invisible and hard to get a hold of; even though you know he has an impact on you." Last, Tom's contemporary Artie plaintively describes how "sometimes Baba rides so fast [in a small vehicle] that I cannot catch up with him."

The children describe this distance with an undercurrent of frustration and helplessness. It seems that they would very much like to be closer to God, and by implication, their fathers as well. It is hard for the boys to understand how a being that is actively involved in their lives can paradoxically remain so aloof—"out there in the sky somewhere," as Tom laments. As with the theme of "active orientation," the motif of God's distance makes us wonder about a deity created in man's image to fulfill unmet paternal needs (Freud 1937). While I speak to this more directly in chapter 7, it is important to delineate the underlying inference. By including these responses in a chapter on sex differences, I mean to suggest that the male sex-role socialization profoundly influences the form and content of deity conceptions. Yet this finding in itself does not explain all conceptions or eradicate, once and for all, the possibility of a more original God.

Identification or Counteridentification

In keeping with this paternal imprint, the children also seem to identify or counteridentify themselves with their deity representations, much as a child might with this father. In this way, the deity serves as something of a role model, an image to strive toward or move away from.

Tom, our twelve-year-old introduced previously, presents a graphic illustration of this theme below. Tom's drawing speaks for itself, an expression of Tom's yearning for a "big man" or father figure that he can emulate. Tom entitles his drawing "God meets the people," and he later explains that God comes down to earth so the people can learn to be like him. In his follow-up story, Tom adds, "God is not really that different than us." Finally, the long-legged, athletic look of the deity is more than serendipitous; it mirrors Tom's own youthful figure and perhaps that of the professional basketball player he would like to grow into.

But not all male children identify so affirmatively with their deity conceptions. Six-year-old Gerard al-

God meets the people. Drawing by twelve-year-old Tom.

ludes to a deity who is against war and anger. Gerard
takes great glee in the aggression of family confronta-
tions while the deity conception does not. Thus a the
commonality across the male children dissipates as
each child becomes engrossed in his own particular
version of identification. Beside this dichotomy of identification and counteridentification, some children demonstrate explicit modeling (e.g., Tom) while others indicate a more subtle and even unconscious process. For
example, eleven-year-old David notes, "The Lord is like
a figure in your mind. . . . And yet, it is important for me
to be myself no matter how I imagine the Lord." Such
identification seems to follow in line with some of the
psychoanalytic literature already cited, as well as more
specific work on the socialization processes of boys
(Rizzuto 1979).

The twofold nature of identification—of identification or counteridentification—is particularly noteworthy given the popularity of the God/Devil motif in our
culture and many others. The God/Devil theme appears
in Gerard's protocol and in several others where there
is an occasional mention of a counterforce ("Satan,"
"bad spirits"). Three possibilities emerge, none of which
are falsifiable.

First, this duality may reflect an ambivalence in the
boys' relationships to their fathers. This is perhaps
close to the interpretation of Sigmund Freud. Antideity
sentiment then would indicate some negative feelings
toward the boys' fathers. Second, the duality may reflect a real assessment of the world, or at least the
child's perspective on the world at large. In other
words, the child develops a conviction that this is a
world of anger as well as love, a world of things to
emulate as well as a world of things to avoid. The deity
conception then, would serve as a metaphor for the
nature of life. Last, in the view of some formal religions
and many individuals, the child in his person bears

some aspect of the divine as well as the profane, or that which is not the divine. What is most intriguing about this view is the resulting difficulty for the child: will identification with an image bring him closer or pull him farther away from God in God's authenticity?

Anxiety Concerning the Idea of a Female God

The last of the major motifs for the male children is probably the least detectable and yet perhaps the most universal among the twenty children. Despite their age and religious differences, the youngsters manifest tremendous anxiety about the thought that this deity might be female. In response to the question "What if the deity is the other sex or both sexes?" and in their spontaneous impressions, these boys seem highly guarded against anything approaching a feminine characteristic in their representations.

Consider for a moment nine-year-old Arthur. Looking bewildered and a bit "out of kilter," Arthur eventually speaks in regard to the "other sex" inquiry:

A: God is a man, for sure.

DH: What if God was the other sex?

A: But God is a man!

DH: But could you play "What if"?

A: If God was a . . . huh! Well, I don't know [laughs anxiously]. I don't know. Well, I couldn't even imagine God being a lady—no sir [laughs nervously].

In Arthur's reactions, he demonstrates a visible investment in a male God, pushing away any thought of a female deity. However, his response, one of surprise and apprehension, does not suggest total unfamiliarity with the idea. Arthur seems to be protesting too much. It seems he knows that people consider the idea but it clearly makes him uncomfortable. And yet strangely for someone who presents himself as befuddled, Arthur elevates this female deity to a high status. She is a "lady," and something about this is scary and unnerving to him.

There are several possible reasons for Arthur and the other boys' anxieties. Among other reasons are the following: (1) an anxiety associated with the mystery of motherhood and womanhood and its impact on the male child; (2) anxiety associated with individual socialization experiences with mothers, although individual personality and family dynamics do not seem to explain adequately the prevalence of this phenomenon; (3) a fear of returning to the all-encompassing womb under the control of a female God and, inversely, a wish for such a return (e.g., Arthur's interest in calling the deity a lady as a sign of some wish); and (4) anxiety about possible happiness associated with a benign female deity rather than a more distant and less benign male deity. It is likely that the individual children will differ in regard to which reasons are most applicable.

On the subject of male apprehension, Wolfgang Lederer wrote *The Fear of Women* (1968). In this work, Lederer colorfully describes the dread and angst that most men experience in regard to feminine control, "as powerful as the sea and as inescapable as fate." Lederer observes that men oscillate eternally between love and fear of feminine impact, though much of the fear and some of the love is often repressed.

The Female Children
An Aesthetic God

In sharp contrast to the rational orientation of their male counterparts, the female participants describe a deity characterized by aesthetic appeal and by investment in the artistic world. Music, dance, and art—all are within the unlimited domain of this God.

Several girls stand out for their individualized representations. Seven-year-old Jeri repeatedly mentions that she thinks of God when she hears "easy music" (i.e., soft music). She voices this in refrain throughout the interview. With her own lyrical style of expression, she made me guess that it might have early childhood roots for her—perhaps the soothing sound of her mother's lullaby in the wake of an absent father. Among others, Jeri's contemporary Hallie reveals a moment of pleasure when she thinks of how "God made my blue eyes just like God made the sky." And nine-year-old Carol, responding to her drawing, comments that she often associated the process of drawing with religious feelings: "Because making pictures and being creative makes me feel so good."

In general, the God representations of the girls are not nearly so grounded in concrete facts and events as are those of the boys. In their depictions, the girls collectively present a deity that is closer to sound and color, closer to nature and natural phenomena, and farther from technical or scientific constructions. Sometimes their aesthetic references appear to be projections of their own aesthetic and feminine qualities passed on to the deity; in other instances no such displacement is readily apparent. On the whole, we might say of the conceptions of the girls that their God is clearly the God who created rainbows. Thus the girls manifest an interesting blend of gender and religious socialization influences.

The aesthetic orientation of the girls is not to be confused with the "aesthetic principle" postulated by Kierkegaard, who suggests a stage of religious development aimed at pleasure seeking alone (Fairchild 1971). The girls' conceptions are more refined and mature, having a quality of shared aesthetic joy with the world at large.

In *Women, Reason, and Nature* (1982), Carol McMillan observes that the aesthetic versus rational division is a primary socialization difference between women and men, perhaps with some biological origins. She relates the investment of women in the aesthetic to a preference for a more feeling-oriented life and a greater tendency toward compassion and expression.

Beyond these theoretical considerations, the girls' aesthetic orientation provides us with an initial glimpse into their view of a possible female God. If in fact the deity might be closer to the earth, closer to nature, and closer to the act of birth, then it is not much farther to believe that this deity is indeed feminine. As we shall see, the girls do entertain this possibility, though not without some reservation and conflict.

Passivity

Passivity is emphasized by the female participants, either as a characteristic of the deity or in human relations with the deity. The deity's activity, even when acknowledged, is not a primary topic of concentration.

Thus sometimes God is very active and the girls focus on their role as the recipients of God's actions. Eight-year-old Miriam describes such a scene in her "child alone" scenario, as the child receives copious gifts from the deity. Seven-year-old Jeri echoes similar sentiments when she too expresses a recurring desire to "receive love" from God. Other children seem to project their passivity onto the deity, so that God becomes a more domestic and even docile figure. As eight-year-old Dina says in her description, "God spends a lot of time just watching from his home in heaven."

Generally, the give-and-take between God and the female children is more verbal and direct; communication between God and the boys is more action oriented. God affects the lives of the girls through their creative endeavors or through their quiet contemplations. God rarely emerges as a burning bush or as an umpire calling the third strike in a little league game. For the girls, the deity is less aggressive and obvious in demeanor, but certainly no less pervasive or significant in communication.

The psychoanalytic view suggests that women are naturally passive. This of course has become quite controversial owing to the possible impact of socialization factors like parental expectations. Concerning passivity as a historically conditioned female trait, Janine Chassequet-Smirgel (1970) writes that the main distinction between men and women is the difference between activity and passivity. Apparently, this common difference, however biological or however learned, represents an overlay on the children's deity conceptions.

A More Intimate God

The girls present a God of at least relative emotional intimacy, in contrast to the more distant God the boys describe. While occasionally the girls stress a physical closeness, most often they refer to the exchange of feelings between God and human beings.

Among other examples, nine-year-old Carin observes that "God is always close by, guiding whatever she does." Similarly, six-year-old Annette comments, "I feel close to the Lord in church and when I pray ... I have a lot of feelings then." Seven-year-old Lauren provided a picture of a smiling God (see below) and added, "God is smiling like when you feel his presence beside you."

Such descriptions are characterized by a God who engages in casual conversation and approaches the girls quite naturally. While not every interaction is highly meaningful, the deity does get close to the child in aspects of her life that are important. Issues of intimacy are viewed by the girls as central, though there are episodes of doubt in relation to erratic intimacy. Above all, the God of the female participants is more intimacy-oriented than power-oriented.

Hans Küng (1979) writes that intimacy is involved in the key realization that God is not merely a figure in the

Drawing by seven-year-old Lauren

sky. Apparently, the girls demonstrate a certain maturity in their religious development through their appreciation for an intimate God, at least according to Küng's view.

Specifically in regard to sex differences, Ulanov (1981) observes that the pronounced concern of women with intimacy represents "a different kind of knowledge," a knowledge of the world that is more relational than purely rational. In this way, Ulanov highlights a contrast between women and men that also seems to find its way into their God representations.

Identification with the Role of Partner to the Deity

The twenty female participants indicate a prevailing interest in the mystery of partnership with the deity. Unlike their male counterparts, who struggle with identification and living in the image of the deity, the girls seem to be concerned with "joining" with this God. While a few indicate the clear influence of religious dogma in this regard (e.g., of the bridegroom parable in Matthew and of the New Testament in general), most suggest that a strong relational orientation results from socialization into the female sex role.

The use of biblical characters to indicate "partnership identification" appears in the protocols of seven-year-old Lauren and eight-year-old Miriam, whose drawing appeared in chapter 3. Lauren, in her story, focuses on Simon in his interactions with Jesus: "Simon and the other disciples were to take care of and pass along the wisdom that Jesus gave them." In Lauren's script, the central character's receptive mode is also apparent; Simon seems almost pregnant with the words of Jesus.

Miriam, in a fashion similar to Lauren, concentrates on the Old Testament figure of Miriam, who appears in Exodus. Miriam notes:

Miriam was a significant person in God's plans in ancient Egypt. As Moses' sister, she was important. ... She received God's inspiration in order to help

Moses [pause, then a beaming look of pride]: My name is like Miriam's . . . I was named after Miriam.

Again, the receptive, helping mode is apparent in Miriam's explanation, and her obvious identification with her namesake in this regard is indisputable. The other children present more subtle examples of a similar nature. Most notable among these other girls is nine-year-old Carol. Apparently a devotee of Freudian theory, Carol volunteers, "God is someone who gives to me, and is almost like another father to me in that way."

These identifications suggest that the girls desire a significant spiritual or even holy role in the course of events, but do not feel quite comfortable in being the main actor in these occurrences. They therefore turn to the roles of secondary characters much more than do the boys. In fact, the girls intimate some anxiety about assuming a greater role, like that role approximating the place of the deity.

Along with this self-proscribed role assignment, the interest in partnership seems to speak to an interest in the father-daughter relationship and, ultimately, in becoming part of a marital dyad. Here the God representation is filled with the presence of a desired male partner, one who allows some mobility despite his superiority.

It does seem that the girls are continuing to evidence learned sex-role behavior in their deity conceptions. In *The Psychology of Women* (1971), a frequently cited contribution in the sex-differences literature, Judith Bardwick argues that little girls are frequently discouraged from assuming primary, instrumental roles, nor do their mothers model such roles. Thus girls are relegated to secondary or subordinate endeavors. If this is so and is emerging in relation to deity conceptions in the abstract sense, it is perhaps more concretely evident in some of the consternation concerning a female president. It is interesting to note that Americans by only a thin majority were comfortable with the notion of a female vice-presidential candidate, who of course is still in a secondary or partnership status.

In discussing the interplay of religion and sex differences, Ann Ulanov simply states, "It has become fundamental to a woman's role to be the recipient (or partner) of other, or of the Other" (1981, 63). Ulanov, in contrast to Bardwick's position, points out that there is a positive function for this socialized sex difference. According to Ulanov, by being so concerned with partnership, even excessively so, women remind everyone of the importance of "otherness," without which there can be no true religion. She offers an interesting position, I think, but Bardwick's well-accepted observations still stand out as the most trenchant statement concerning the theme of partnership.

Surface Masculinity/Latent Androgyny

The four themes we have discussed no doubt imply that the girls, too, present a physically male deity conception. What is less apparent but still emergent in the girls' responses is a more androgynous conception, an image that the girls harbor but are hesitant to put forth bluntly. A more androgenous conception, or even a largely feminine one, emerges spontaneously from the political attitudes of female group members when I asked them, "Could the deity be the other sex?"

In response to this question, seven year-old Jeri observed, "Usually, he is a man. But some people think he could be a woman, with long hair and all. I don't see why he always has to be a man." Six year-old Edith, more indignant than Jeri, delivers back immediately, "Of course, God could be female! God could be both!" For eight-year-old Dina and nine-year-old Carin, the deity is passive, aesthetically oriented, and partner oriented. But physically, their God conceptions remain masculine. Dina and Carin are not wholly comfortable with a more androgynous image, but nonetheless the latent inclination exists in their scripts.

For most of the female children, this androgynous element emerges upon persistent inquiry. But how can we explain the differences between the girls and boys in this regard? I think a plausible consideration is that both sexes have an underlying tendency toward androgyny. Each is essentially uncomfortable with it; the boys manifesting their anxiety through a rigid denial and rejection, the girls through keeping their imagery latent and unexpressed. As twelve-year-old Lorraine acknowledges, "I believe that God may have a little of both sexes but I'm afraid to say this out loud. . . . I guess 'cause people might think I'm stupid or something." Lorraine's trepidation seems to me to speak to a common fear of both boys and girls, that somehow their more original ideas concerning God and sexuality may be criticized. Somehow, we hope, Lorraine's honesty will eventually carry the day with her apparently skeptical friends and family.

The concept of androgyny has in some ways been part of psychology since Carl Jung's theory of male and female archetypes (Lips and Colwill 1978). Contemporary psychology offers a view of mastery styles that suggests androgyny is indeed part of everyone; it seems to emerge most prominently in mid life, but not necessarily at the same point for men and women. Robert Stoller (1972) makes the point that sexual orientation owes a great deal to early socialization and to family dynamics. Judging by the protocols of the female participants, this certainly could be true of the expression of the various sides of sexuality, particularly as it influences religious conceptions.

Epilogue: Sex Differences

The forty children, divided equally among boys and girls, show clear sexual socialization imprints on their deity conceptions. Isolating the factor of sex highlights the pervasive age-old tendency for God to appear as a "great father," and for children to impose their paternal-related needs on their conceptions. When one looks deeper into the children's responses, some alternative conceptions briefly emerge. Given this important impact of sexual socialization, it seems likely that continuing changes in sex-role norms in our society may influence the God representations of future generations.

6

Personality Themes

Dear Distant God,
I want to call heaven, but I don't think I'll
be allowed. Would you take a collect call?

Anonymous

The fourth socialization concern is the most individual
and the most influential. The personality configuration
of the child runs through every aspect of his or her life.
Sometimes it seems that personality represents the
child—personality and child are inseparable. Yet personality, however constant ordinarily, is subject to
change through life events. This capacity for change
speaks to its influence by socialization.

The following typologies are not personality dimensions per se but personality orientations in regard to a
deity, the likely consequences of personal style, attitude, and development, along with temperament. These
traits may be projected upon or transfigured into a
personal deity. There is perhaps an infinite array of
such possible conceptions. I am presenting here, for the
sake of highlighting key themes, the personality types
that appear most commonly among my forty young
interviewees.

The Children's Types
God, the Friendly Ghost

One of the most prominent and easily discernible God-
types, which suggests a particular personality of the

child, is the "friendly God." The friendly God usually appears as a congenial spirit that befriends the child and engages in peerlike intervention and play. The deity is similar to an imaginary playmate; the relationship between child and God is lighthearted and enjoyable.

The friendly God is casual and relaxed, even humorous, though it sometimes lacks substance or depth in its relationships. A child with a friendly God usually shows little interest or investment in historical or world events and tends to steer clear of negative sentiment or doubt. Thus children in this personality group respond with enthusiasm to the fun and changes questions, but with less fervor to the death questions. Their deity is an inhabitant of the land of simplicity and is drawn to the small things in life. Its essentially human interpersonal manner stands in contrast to its ethereal and spiritlike nature, a conflict in the child himself or herself.

One such child of the friendly God is ten-year-old Lenny. Even at the outset of interviewing, Lenny demonstrated a quiet and tranquil demeanor. He was pleasant and, as befit his God representation, genuinely friendly. Our relationship remained polite and affable throughout, as his concluding letter suggests:

Dear God,
    I think that Mr. Heler is nice and I had a good time tonight. I did good in math today. How's your math? Jon [another friend] and I worked together in art.

                                                    Lenny

This personality posture, characterized by a steady simplification of life right down to the oversimplification of my last name, also overlays Lenny's depictions of the deity. In his drawing below, Lenny offers a portrait of an apparition smiling gently and surrounded by symbols of sunshine and peace. In the family sce-

Drawing by ten-year-old Lenny

nario, God and family play a board game together. In the "child alone" scenario, God and the little boy discuss the possibility of getting a family pet, a cat that will serve as the boy's companion. The most revealing part of the interview, the segment in which Lenny speaks as much about himself as his God, ensues in his description of the deity: "He's a nice, friendly person . . . and I think he'll do things for other people . . . not big things. . . . But he's usually good about things. He's just a plain, good kind of person."

Lenny and other children like him demonstrate an inner world which calls for friendship and for a sense of peaceful playfulness. The children are reasonably happy, but nonetheless a certain degree of loneliness stands alongside their pleasantness and goodness.

The importance of imaginary playmates for many children, and particularly for "only children" like Lenny, is well documented in developmental literature (Chrenka 1983). Such fantasy characters frequently provide for a safe and happy world and thus insulate the child from the fears of a less placid existence. Above and beyond this, such characters act as friendly companions who fill a void in the child's life or compensate for "less than friendly" siblings and friends. The influence of these qualities on deity forms is thus not particularly surprising. This God-type even occurs in secondary status in the protocols of children with somewhat different personalities.

In *Children's Friendships* (1980), Zick Rubin emphasizes the "wished for" aspect of positive fantasy conceptions, whether they are superheroes, fairies, avatars, or gods. Rubin also stresses that things usually go very smoothly for the child with such figures, even if they exist precisely because some events go awry in real life. And Rubin also comments on the common appearance of friendly characters and imaginary friendships, as he offers an explanation relevant for a friendly God:

> Friendships are among the central ingredients of children's lives, from as early as age three—or, in some cases, even earlier, through adolescence. Friendships occupy, both in their actual conduct

and in the world of thought and fantasy, a large proportion of children's waking hours. (1980, 95)

In Lenny's case, it seems that his deity conception assures him of a friendly world; yet it does not help him appreciate complexity in the world. Clearly, fun and play are prominent in Lenny's waking thoughts, though their exclusivity limits his world view, and perhaps his drive for personal discovery as well.

God, the Angry Villain

In sharp contrast to this benign, friendly deity, a significant group of children carry a deity consumed by rage and villainy. These children describe a larger-than-life deity, who lashes out uncontrollably when angered. Sometimes this God acts sadistically, but always, this God acts arbitrarily and with little sincere compassion. The youngsters either live in fear or manage to grow accustomed to and accommodate this wickedly powerful deity. And, as one might logically anticipate, there is more than a hint of an overbearing and destructive parent in the lives and words of these children.

The Angry Villain is frequently the incarnation of evil, an amalgam of authoritarianism and rage. It occasionally appears under the banner of "Anti-God" or "Satan" but is thus constructed by the child to present some negative sense of a deity. While the deity shares some power characteristics in common with other God-types, this angry version is epitomized by the aggressive impulse.

In keeping with its aggressive nature, the angry deity conception is self-centered and seeks only its own security and enhancement. Guided by greed, it evidences little concern for other people or for its child-creator. It sometimes uses threat or induces guilt to achieve desired ends; the child is rendered helpless in the wake of these manipulations. In the end, the children describe this deity in great detail during their interviews and then, quite naturally, seem vigilant or avoidant in reaction to it.

In the language of formal religion, the angry God is truly the God of thunderbolts, lightning, and floods— not the God of peace and justice. Frequently associated with war (i.e., starting and not stopping), this deity is intimately involved in animosity and tension between people. This auxiliary theme emerges most lucidly in family play scenarios. The children's scripts suggest that the angry God grows from harsh and one-sided parenting. As a result, the children maintain in their small persons an inordinate amount of rage, which they partially project onto the deity. Thus the God image allows for a certain release of aggression at the same time it keeps child and parent relatively safe from forbidden aggressive impulses. If the anger is "out there" in the deity, the child reasons, "then it cannot be as strong in me or in my parents." Unfortunately, this clever fantasy maneuver does not sufficiently protect the child from an angry God.

Six-year-old Gerard is an example of a child with a negative deity representation. Gerard's oppositional demeanor and villainous portrayal of God went hand-in-hand as he conveyed some of his terribly difficult inner life. It was evident that he and his God were not going to be friendly when I began the naming portion of the introduction. Asked to give a name or label to his representations, Gerard exclaimed indignantly, "God ... I said God, damn it! I call it God—and I'm only answering questions if I want to." In general, a careless, bitter tone was the accompaniment to Gerard's responses and outbursts.

Storytelling introduced us to some similar aggression surrounding the deity conception for Gerard. In discussing God's preferred activities, Gerard matter-offactly observes, "The President and God had a war ... and they used weapons like swords and chains, chains with those round things with prickles." Gerard seems to be capturing here some familiar battle with his father, as well as some purely internal cataclysm of his own. These wartime, tension-filled scenes continued throughout his family scenarios. When God enters a scene, even theatrical sets that are already overflowing with tension and discord, characters mysteriously grow ill or die, usually in an excruciatingly painful manner. Gerard's aggression proceeds uninterrupted into his response to the question about God's activities. He simply shouts, "God just has wars! I think he is a sergeant." (Gerard does not want to give this deity, and symbolically his father, a high rank.) Finally, he explains the consequences of disobedience of the deity—"Traitors are left out in the desert"—indicating his fears and his self-imposed banishment from positive strivings.

Perhaps more than any other child, Gerard graphically and painfully illustrates how personality neuroses can overtake and blacken a deity conception. Certainly, family tensions and anger are most intrusive in his interview responses. Specifically, venomous relations are most pronounced between and among male characters. Of such angry children, Fritz Redl writes a classic piece from the perspective of clinical psychology, in which he calls this phenomenon the appearance of "a mislaid Santa Claus. With no concept of a truly benign spirit, even the best of fantasy or real imagery can be ruined" (1951, 34).

But why is Gerard's God so unduly and so relentlessly angry? The possibility must be considered that God is angry because of some perceived wrongdoing on Gerard's part, a forbidden wish or act. In other words, the deity representation is Gerard's judge and executioner, the natural creation of his excessive guilt. In fact, Gerard does evidence pervasive guilt throughout the protocol, especially as a result of any hint of sexuality or in regard to some overt aggression. So for Gerard, a relationship between the angry God and guilt is a real possibility. Concerning this pattern of guilt, the resulting need for punishment, and the emergence of an angry figure, Carole Klein writes most cogently and, I think, speaks to some part of Gerard's troublesome concerns:

> For it [guilt in a child] does, chameleonlike, take on many, sometimes ingeniously disguised forms. . . . Nightmares, along with a nightmarish number of daytime fears, are often the creations of a punishing conscience. (1975, 128)

God, the Distant Thing in the Sky

A third orientation, one which brings together children of both diffident and highly avoidant personalities, presents a nebulous deity far from the crowds and concerns of the child's everyday life.

The distant God is experienced by the child as real but existing in a realm very far removed. This God is elusive and cloaked in psychical and psychological uncertainty. Frequently, it is associated with "heaven," "space," or, most often, "the sky." In the child's renditions, there is little emotional exchange between deity and humankind, and the child intimates that such distance is universal.

Distance is the sine qua non of this deity. Thus the drawings of these children recede into the background; characters in scenarios are somewhat vague and nonintimate, and the relationship that develops between child and interviewer is also reserved. Throughout the interview responses, the God figure is surrounded by ambiguity, an inexplicable vagueness that surpasses the cognitive confusion of any particular age group. Life goes on in predictable fashion in stories and scenarios, but the God figure is essentially uninvolved and unimportant. Often, there are subtle indications that the child wishes to be closer to this deity, but he or she quickly writes off the idea. It is as if such intimacy is considered unattainable, impossible with the distant God. These personality qualities are typified by five-year-old Keith. Keith's central figure is equated with deceased relatives that Keith has never met. "I think about God and my relatives," Keith says in response to the naming question and makes reference to the Holocaust victims in his family. The two images of reference, deity and deceased relatives, seem related for Keith in some other, faraway space and time. It is a realm that he cannot reach.

The notion of distance continues to arise spontaneously from Keith. Throughout, he expresses a fear that we will not have enough time because the interviewer will have to go away soon. But there are specific distance images in the discussion of the deity too. "God lives in a bed of clouds," Keith informs us. Later, he poignantly transforms his earlier description: "God is just a cloud." And still later in the interview, he utters, "I'm not clear about too much about God." In regard to everyday activities, Keith's God shows little relation to or involvement with earthly matters. Finally, in his letters, Keith reveals a yearning for some seemingly impossible tryst:

Dear God,
    I wish I could meet you and my relatives.

Love,
Keith

The parent imagery of Keith and similarly styled children, as indicated by their stories, scenarios, and responses, reflects a tremendous amount of interpersonal distance between spouses and between each parent and child. These families are largely disengaged, each individual actor moving around in an independent and unrelated orbit. While the God representations of these children are not clearly parental figures per se, family relations and their absence do place a thick lining over the God representation that is virtually impossible to remove.

What stands out and underlies these children's inner worlds is a tremendous sense of loneliness, a loneliness that Keith movingly suggests in reference to our time together. In *The Myth of the Happy Child* (1975), Carole Klein speaks of the great difficulty children have in expressing and in confronting their loneliness. Like the imaginary or real figures they may seek, the loneliness itself is confusing and elusive. Sometimes a neutral or distant figure evolves, a result of the child's creative energy in spite of emptiness. According to Keith's responses, even a bland, unappealing figure may be preferable to loneliness.

The distant God may be such a neutrally toned figure. It does seem to serve two related functions for Keith and some other children: (1) it occupies at least part of the formidable void in the child's life, and (2) it also gives lifelike expression to the painful sense of estrangement that the children inwardly experience.

God, the Lover in Heaven

Some of the children demonstrate a highly romanticized notion of a deity, a beloved who serves as a partner in passionate love. This theme is more common among girls, but appears in the imagery of two boys as well.

This deity appears as a kind of mate or spouse. God has the qualities of Sir Lancelot, Don Juan, and Casanova all in one. As an eternal bride or bridegroom, the deity is highly eroticized and sexualized and always provides exciting companionship. God is the object or fountain of much yearning, but the sexual component causes much anxiety and reluctance. There appears to be a great drive toward the deity, but equally, much fear of the enticing image.

By inference, it seems that this God representation builds on unusually intense relations with a parent of the opposite sex. Such relationships trigger tremendous yearning as well as memory traces of profound gratification and happiness. At least partially, God then comes to represent the wish for reunification with such a parent and the fruition of the unfulfilled promises of the parent.

This interpersonal landscape of love and yearning is epitomized by nine-year-old Carin. Through her engaging manner and gentle coquettishness, Carin related to me from the outset as a peer and treated me like a romantic interest. Her desire to blur our age difference was, in part, successful, and I felt at times that I was with a young adult.

But this interpersonal style was but a precursor for her interview responses. In Carin's drawing below, the young artist reveals a handsome, debonair, even swashbuckling man. He is neither oversized nor receding, but seems in his prime and is decidedly male. In her story about this romantic figure, Carin giggles nervously as God enters and leaves the shower. A female character awaits his exit so that she can bestow a gift, the nature of which is left histrionically unclear.

In family scenarios, the scene is adorned with flower bouquets and boxes of chocolate. God is more of a giver and recipient than an authority figure or symbol of conscience. Throughout Carin's protocol, physical attractiveness is emphasized, as with her response to how God lives:

God's home is beautiful. It is well decorated. . . It's great. [Laughs nervously, as if discussing a forbidden topic] But I don't really know for sure.

Drawing by nine-year-old Carin

At the end of her response, Carin draws away from her God out of anxiety. This leaves her with a certain yearning, a yearning which emerges most graphically when she is moved to tears near the end of the inter-

view: "I love him so much I can't explain it in words."
While also a source of joy, it seems that the "lover God"
is the origin of some pain for Carin as well.

Concerning the opposite-sex parent and "lover" sym-
bolism, the Simone de Beauvoir writes of her own life
and the deification of her father with words that well
describe Carin's view:

> [In my eyes], it is through him that the family
> communicates with the rest of the world: he incar-
> nates that immense, difficult, and marvelous world
> of adventure; he personifies transcendence, he is
> God. (1968, 154)

The Inconsistent God

A significant set of children describe a most quixotic
deity, a representation defined by its very twofoldness.
This God conception is unpredictable and undepend-
able. While it does take the form of a positive force on
occasion, it can also work insidiously against the child
and thus causes great ambivalence.

It is the tendency to oscillate from helper to hinderer
that marks the presence of the inconsistent God. In the
eyes of the child, good and evil transpire episodically
and the inconsistency of life is difficult to understand.
The resulting conflict about the deity is often evident,
though negative feelings are not always openly acknowledged or consciously entertained. Such a conception, images of an alternately positive and then negative God, seems to typify the children's parent
representations as well. In their implications and responses to parent-related questions, these children picture their parents as "in-and-out," available and yet
unavailable to the child.

While inconsistency is a secondary trait in many of
the children's conceptions, it is a primary characteristic
of several, including twelve-year-old Artie. Artie's in-

terview is conducted with a concentration on "Baba," his representation of a deity. But Artie shows a bit of confusion about whether Baba is only a person or an actual deity; this highlights his sense of an unpredictable God. The relevant imagery surfaces during Artie's drawing, when he initially begins to draw Baba and then elects to depict "another person, instead."

In Artie's story and scenarios, Baba provides desired gifts and rewards but not always in desired fashion. For example, in his story Artie is given a lollipop by Baba. But rather than hand it to Artie gently, Baba thrusts it into Artie's mouth so hard that Artie nearly gags. The denial of negative feelings is readily apparent when Artie abruptly ends his story:

> The pop was great! [not said with conviction]. Um
> ... well, it was ... er ... Can I tell another story?
> [said anxiously].

Artie's mixed picture and mixed feelings come to a critical juncture when he discusses faith and doubt. Putting his own sentiments into the words of another religious follower, Artie wonders about Baba's falsehood. "He was so nice sometimes, but not always, the man would say.... Was Baba God; was he so perfect?" It seems that the deity and its inconsistency has rendered Artie confused and doubtful. While he learns much more on the side of belief and positive regard, Artie experiences conflictual feelings that he continues to struggle with.

In an informative article entitled "The Bruised Self" (1972), Kirkhart and Kirkhart discuss the phenomenon of inconsistent caretaking and its long-term impact on the world view of the child. The authors describe how some parent and parent surrogates can be intermittently accepting and rejecting and how respective parents can offer different messages. The result can be a most disturbing and circular chain of events for the child; the child's distress at adult inconsistency is exacerbated by the anger the child has come to expect for his failure to please. (1972) A child like Artie who does strive to please is left confused. He is left angry and perhaps guilty about his underlying negative feelings. Faced with a world dominated by the inconsistent God, it is difficult for a child to know which way to turn.

God, the Once and Future King

For a number of children, God appears as the head of the government of the universe. Occupying a royal position, God makes general laws and dispenses justice among the inhabitants of earth. While he possesses the absolute right of a king, most of the children report that he administers his power with thoughtfulness and mercy. As a result of these unparalleled responsibilities, God has the quality of a "super big man"—not so much in the purely heroic sense but in the spirit of one who is at the pinnacle of universal power.

As an exceedingly powerful figure, this deity conception is neither extremely loving or particularly vengeful. It is, however, indisputably dominant and frequently male in characterization. In regard to its activities, the deity is eminently and actively involved in the geopolitical affairs of the world. It demonstrates a greater inclination for intervention in universal history than for involvement in individual lives, though both are within God's global domain.

In regard to relationships, the deity seems to have a similar liaison with Jesus as with, say, President Reagan. These human figures are considered by the children to be lieutenants of God. Parents occupy a related status as communicators of God's message. In actuality, the parents of these children, and the fathers in particular, are strikingly controlling and powerful though not dictatorial or truly authoritarian. These fathers show a genuine though sometimes self-absorbed caring for the children, unlike the parents of children who describe an angry God. "God, the King," is exemplified by twelve-year-old Tom. We have already seen Tom's drawing of a big and dominant man in chapter 5. Yet his other interview reactions elaborate on the themes suggested by his drawing. In play scenarios, Tom emphasizes that "God is perfect and this is why he has so much power, because people are not perfect." In his Description, God is "a big, gigantic person" who has "hundreds of angels" as his subjects. In his activities, God emerges as "a great decisionmaker who controls fate." Finally, in the "famous persons" segment of the interview, Tom adopts an authoritative tone and explains:

> God and Jesus are in charge of different divisions. God is the boss and director of everything . . . Jesus is more involved with people in a flesh and blood way.

For Tom and other children of similar personality, the God image seems to center around the father representation but surpasses this paternal conception. It is similar to the conception of "president" but represents more than this conception in its magnitude and scope. The responses of this group of children are reminiscent of the reactions of children following the assassination of John Kennedy, when they seemed to be seeking an infallible and even higher authority figure (Wolfenstein 1964). Such a figure, like Tom's representation, is clearly a Being that will take charge and keep the known world intact, if also unchanged and unfree.

God, the Therapist (Dr. God)

A concluding personality type, traversing religious, age, and sex differences, suggests a healing deity. This God appears as an all-nurturant, loving figure who rights all of the wrongs of the family and of the world.

God makes everything "okay" for the child, too, and sometimes does so through miraculous means. The central characteristic of this deity is the ability to improve things—the life of the child, the parental relationship, or the state of international relations. Above all, God mends injuries, both physical and emotional though God's full involvement with injuries is not always clear. God's healing emphasis makes the relationship between God and man asymmetrical. While God undertakes ameliorative measures, people return their thanks but are charged with no more than this. By subtle implication, these children convey something of a passive stance, dependent upon "Dr. God."

Eleven-year-old Laura provides a good example of a child of this personality type. In family scenarios, mother, father, and the little girl are sick and God makes them feel better. In her Description, Laura's only responses are the following adjectives: "forgiving, loving, caring." In answering the question about the deity and fun, she notes her thankfulness that God improves the quality of her life: "Like on Thanksgiving, he makes it possible for the whole family to get together and not think about bad times." Clearly, there is a therapeutic emphasis in Laura's concentration on relief from suffering.

The "therapist God" conception is epitomized by Laura's letter, which reads as follows:

Dear God,

I thank you for your loving and caring heart. I wish you would help all the poor and sick of the world. And make it so the whole world will be able to make peace all over. And please help me, too.

Laura

This type of child personality and resulting God figure naturally stem from families which stress therapistlike qualities. Quite often, there is some major pain, injury, or accumulation of suffering. In Laura's case, a younger sister died in a car accident five years ago. At the same time, there is family strength and faith and an apparent capacity to cope with stress. Laura's reasonable optimism is a sign of such strength. Regarding this tolerant, therapeutic stance in the child, Martin and Westee (1972) suggest a common familial pattern. Children who verbalize and manifest such qualities identify more compellingly with nurturant mothers rather than authoritarian or disciplinarian fathers. Laura's mention of her mother, a depiction of a sacrificing saint who takes care of things in the manner of "Dr. God," illustrates the prototypal parent-child relationship.

Epilogue: Personality Themes

Along with other socialization considerations, a child's personality gives a particular form to God conceptions that develop in a number of popular ways. Here we have described the most representative of these forms for the forty children interviewed. Of course, there are a plethora of others, owing to the uniqueness and diversity of human personality.

We now conclude the socialization themes indicated by the four major areas—religion, age, sex, and personality. But we have cause to wonder how these themes come together in the individual child; what accounts for their socialization and relative acceptance by the child? The family concerns of the child's inner world, and by implication his outer world, are thus the focus of the discussion that follows.

The Family: A Socialization Scenario

> *Dear God,*
> *My name is Robert. I want a baby brother.*
> *My mother said to ask my father. My father*
> *said to ask you. Do you think you can do it?*
> *Good luck.*
>
> *Robert*

In writing of children's views of religion and other serious matters, like life and death, Rose Zeligs writes, "A child absorbs the facts in his home from the moment he is born" (1974, 73). While other institutions like church or state do indeed play a role in religious socialization, the family interprets scripture and stricture and seems to act as the final and most influential socializer of religious imagery. It is, after all, in the family that much formal religious dogma and ritual are first introduced. And it is in the family too that much of a child's personal growth is nurtured or arrested. For young children, the small theologians from ages four to twelve, family members are likely to be primary socializers because of their immediacy and because of their essential involvements as caretakers and role models.

God: The Family Portrait
The Father Image

The essence of paternal imagery in a God representation is passionately captured by Edmund Gosse in *Father and Son: A Study of Two Temperaments*:

My mother always deferred to my father, spoke to
me as if he were all-wise. I confused him in some
sense with God; at all events I believed that my
father knew everything and saw everything. [And
then on learning otherwise,] the shock to me was
that of a thunderbolt, for what my father had said
was not true. (1909, 102)

As Gosse implies, the perennial idea has been that God
and father are somehow fused together and the result is
tremendous confusion for the child. The paternal imprint is clearly the most frequently occurring family
influence. It lays claim to children of diverse backgrounds and emerges most noticeably, as we have already indicated, in regard to the socialization of sex
differences.

Certainly, paternal imagery is evident in the protocols of those children, such as twelve-year-old Tom, who
describe a "Once and Future King." Such a God leaves
a definite impression of occupying the head of the
human household. It provides structure and performs
conventionally paternal functions. Selected other sets
of children also indicate a paternal God, judging by the
various executive and quasi-authoritative tasks of their
deities. The Baptist children, with their concern with
order, are one such example. Another manifestation
develops among the female children, with their pronounced wish to receive the God figure and thus, by
implication, their fathers. The male children, too, both
through "big man drawings" and their ambivalent
identification with God as father surrogate, indicate
that fathers are very much in their respective if not
collective unconsciouses. "To be like daddy or not to
be"—that is frequently the question that the boys confront on the level of the God representation. Such
socialization themes point unmistakably to the influence of paternal forms on children's conceptions of God.

Yet even within the realm of socialization and the family, other forms of the deity emerge alongside the father form and these too seem significant for the children. These other forms contribute to the socialized shaping of the representation and determine how religion, age, and sex come together in the individual child's conception. By their very existence, these other forms demonstrate that the formation of a God image is more complex and less easily explained than some writers have allowed.

The Mother Image

The second most prominent image among the children is a maternal image, which has been overlooked in much of the religious development literature—probably because its socialization effects may be less pervasive in a male-oriented society.

Many children indicate, however, that maternal imagery is sufficiently in their inner worlds to direct or guide the course of deity imagery. In contrast to the theme of order, the Baptist participants also express a yearning for nurturance, as classically a maternal element as any. In articulating such yearning, the children describe a softer, warmer deity. This deity becomes the protective cushion of the universe and provides for the child. While it emerges most clearly for the girls, the nurturance theme also surfaces periodically and cautiously in the responses of the boys. Among other religious groups of children, the Catholic participants suggest a maternal element with their "forgiving" theme, which also stirs the notion of an all-embracing mother figure.

The mother image is perhaps most evident among children of the "therapist God" personality type. In their imagery, the corrective, therapeutic touch of the deity is that of a divine mother bandaging their wounds. The absolute, benign quality of this conception overshadows other elements in the children's imagery—particularly those forces, perhaps paternal in origin, that loom as more foreboding to the child. Of course not all maternal imagery is so benign. Ten-year-old Annette of the Baptist group was one of the few children to indicate a mother image in her drawing. Annette seems to depict a more severe, harsh, and controlling maternal figure. Her drawing of her deity appears below.

Several observers have previously noted the preponderance of maternal imagery within individual God representations. Rizzuto (1979), who speaks convincingly concerning Sigmund Freud's neglect of feminine religious imagery, points out that among even conventional religions there is much reference to the sensate and the aesthetic, classically feminine domains. Erik Erikson (1964) also postulates that religious belief seems to have a vital foundation in the early mother-child relationship.

In a rare interview-based research study among children, Godin and Hallez (1964) report the presence of a maternal component in religion-related representations. Interestingly, they note the appearance and then periodic disappearance of the maternal element during the ebb and flow of childhood. Godin and Hallez suggest that sex-role socialization and developmental period interact to determine the visibility of maternal imagery. It seems that boys manifest such representations in more pronounced fashion, a finding consistent with the latent nature of a feminine God in our study among the male children. The girls, on the other hand, evidence clear maternal imagery earlier, and the end of adolescence apparently brings with it much paternal interest.

In earlier noninterview studies, where only questionnaires were utilized, Strunk (1959) and Nelson and Jones (1957) both try to test empirically the Freudian hypothesis of a deity, which sees all God imagery as a

Drawing by ten-year-old Annette

paternal derivative. Both investigations conclude that the maternal element may in fact be stronger in overt imagery and thus that paternal representations are not an underlying universal among individuals.

The Couple Image

A third familial image among the children, one apparently more pervasive than any prior literature has noted, is the image of the deity as a parental couple. While some tasks may naturally elicit such imagery (e.g., the "parents alone" scenario), couple conceptions appear in all segments of the children's protocols. This is not surprising when we consider that children are so much under the auspices of the parental unit; the unhappy child is at the mercy of the parental couple as well.

One of the most memorable reactions of a few children was their obvious joy (and accompanying anxiety) during the "parents alone" scenario. A brief glimpse of their facial expressions, their exuberance, revealed what must have been their prevailing thought: "Now, the roles are reversed!" Now the children would get to play God rather than live in the world created by their Godlike parents. As four-year-old Marci exclaimed, "This is fun. I wish I could do this all the time!"

But couple imagery abounds in the children's responses to other inquiries as well. The youngest group of children, ages four to six, and the oldest group, ages nine to twelve, imply some element of a split parental conception, as if two external forces need to be reconciled. In other words, both mother and father must be appeased in the deity world of some children. This phenomenon appears with less regularity among the middle age-group, perhaps another indication that they are adjusting to being outside of the parental dyad.

Couple imagery also resides implicitly in the suppressed androgyny of the female children. These children subtly bestow upon the deity the qualities of both sexes. At the same time that they may be giving expression to contrasting sides of themselves, they also provide illustration of the contrariety in the parental dyad. Particularly when some issue of authority is at work, the child presents a God who is involved with combined parental characteristics. For example, ten-year-old Irma says concerning conversation with the deity:

> Yes, it is possible to have a talk. He talks to you when you are thinking about something. He'll give you support and guidance, but also tells you when you're doing something wrong. He does both.

In Irma's inner world, the more maternal "support and guidance" are granted equal time with the more paternal sense of direction. Each quality seems to go hand-in-hand to constitute Irma's deity at this point in her life.

It is also important to mention that Catholic children evidence a great deal of this imagery, owing to their emphasis on marriage and family. Here the intactness of the parental unit is earnestly and religiously protected. In the responses of the Catholic children, the couple image is particularly powerful as a socializing influence.

There exists only very limited attention elsewhere to the couple theme, as well as a sense of the deity as "family." Rizzuto is one of the few writers to comment, though she does only in generalizing from the interview of a single, adult woman. Her observations echo some of what we have observed:

> The question emerges of why the parental couple became the source of many of the elements that form the God representation. . . . The answer [in this one case, but perhaps in others] seems to lie in the fact that the parents formed a symbiotic unit, almost in opposition to the children. (1979, 165).

Such a case is perhaps an extreme example, but

Rizzuto's underlying inference, that parents can profoundly shape the God conception by their manner as a couple, is quite consistent with my own.

The Grandparent Image

Another motif demonstrated by the children is the archetypal grandparent—a wise and trustworthy figure who somehow has greater status or knowledge than the child's parents. The grandparent deity may be one sex or the other and is usually in the same image as the parental figures, but the grandparent deity is less involved in authority and discipline. While this family theme is evident in the children's responses, it is less pronounced in individual children than one might anticipate. Perhaps as a result of increased social mobility, the children see their grandparents infrequently and thus the potential effects of their grandparents are less developed.

The children occasionally bring in grandparent imagery spontaneously in family scenarios and always by direction in the question about God and "famous figures." For example, in both interview segments, some of the children with "therapist God" personalities emphasize characteristics like wisdom and understanding and associate this with God's advanced age. The Jewish children, in keeping with their investment in history, sometimes bestow the deity with qualities of their past and immediate ancestors. Other children, across religious groups, invoke grandparent imagery when they seem displeased with their parents or their parents seem imperfect. Grandparent figures are apparently seen as impeccable and as arbiters of parent-child difficulties. As eleven-year-old Becky Sue says, "God is a little like my grandfather. . . . He smiles a lot and fixes toys for you when you need him to."

Several writers have speculated that the frequent occurrence of grandparent imagery may reflect a time of transition, as children begin to depart somewhat from the nuclear family (Rizzuto 1979). However, it seems equally plausible that a grandparent God may reflect an actual and extensive involvement of a grandmother or grandfather.

The Wished-for or Feared Parent Image

An additional inspiration for the deity image may be fantasy imagery woven by the child in response to the family and displaced onto a concept like "God." The God concept then becomes a convenient surrogate and cognomen for sensitive material. We know that a central process involved in fantasy play is "repetition"—a child's inclination to replay and transform experiences to improve his or her condition in the home and master a situation (Chrenka 1983). It seems that such repetition is at work (or, more accurately, at play) as the child depicts characters who are given life by parent-related wishes and fears.

The wished-for parent and father is implicit in the representation of "God, the Once and Future King." In particular, the male children in this personality group seem to want to grant a father greater power than he actually has. Such a conception also can reflect for either sex a wish for the father to be king. Then, the child imagines, he or she can inherit royalty and assume a rightful place as prince or princess. It is perhaps not serendipitous that twelve-year-old Tom, the author of the "big man" drawing, volunteers that the musical celebrity Prince is one of his idols.

Other wished-for themes are indicated by the Catholic group's emphasis on "forgiving" and the "friendly God" group's responses. In such cases, the children seem to be seeking a more benign overseer, as well as an internalized conscience that will treat them more gently. They wish for a conscience free from harsh standards and judgment and filled with greater tolerance and acceptance. For children of the friendly God, the deity also embodies the wished-for friend or comrade, the playmate who represents a panacea for the reality of childhood loneliness.

The feared parent rears its inelegant countenance in a number of socialization groups, including the children of the angry God and the inconsistent God. With these themes, the children demonstrate how parental faults can be particularly destructive as they are seen from the perspective of the child. The angry father becomes the incarnation of evil as he shouts at the child for failing to answer a question. The inconsistent mother assumes the status of a beguiling witch who turns without warning upon the child.

In the child's small magnifying glass, negative feelings and punishment can take on a huge life of their own unless tempered with compassion. Charles Shultz has immortalized this phenomenon in the comic strip "Peanuts," as Charlie Brown and his small cohorts repeatedly hear the words of adults as resounding orders or bellicose screeching. Exaggeration, then, is the essence of the feared-parent influence on the children's deity conceptions. The fantasized parent or God, however, is no less real to the child.

Thus positive, negative, and ambivalent God figures are all part of the family picture, as they suggest fantasy representations triggered by actual parenting. The question naturally arises as to why negative imagery should persist despite their frightening content for children. It is perhaps easier to understand the great strength of the wished-for parent than the insidious lifespan of the feared parent. In *The Uses of Enchantment* (1976), Bruno Bettelheim provides a helpful explanation. Bettelheim, in his most comprehensive analysis of children's fantasy images, observes that fantasy characters help a child attempt to master a difficult situation. In keeping with its repetition function, play

also grants a child the opportunity to master and over-
come. Such gods, as well as monsters and devils, help
children to know and confront the perceived monsters
in their families, and the monsters the children feel or
fear themselves to be.

Epilogue: The Family

The essential idea concerning a God representation and
the family is the tremendous socialization impact of the
family on the formation of this representation. The
impact is longstanding and sometimes even lifelong in
nature. For certain, the indelible influence of family is
highly apparent in the words and actions of our children. Family effects are evident as parents interpret
formal religion, as parents express their own particular
world view, and as they minister to the growth of the
child.

   Yet while family socialization is so pervasive, this
does not necessarily mean it shapes or constitutes a God
conception in its entirety. Family and the various socialization phenomena that are filtered through family
help to explain many of the nuances of children's inner
worlds. From their playful excursions in the sun to
their more serious ruminations in their darkest private
caverns, some layer or layers of family socialization are
discernible. However, there are aspects of the children's
God that are not so easily explained by institutions and
family alone. There are some themes which, though
branded with a certain socialization process, are strikingly universal. These are themes rising out of the
pages of all forty children's protocols, distinguished by
their very persistence and consistency despite clearly
marked socialization differences. These common
themes thus represent the culmination of our exploration of the children's God.

8

Common Themes

Dear God,
 How do you feel about people who don't
believe in you? Somebody else wants to
know.

A Friend,
Neil

One of the principle goals of my whole enterprise with
the children was to determine whether some characteristics of a deity might transcend socialization expectations. I have planned and presented the preceding
chapters in an effort to describe these socialization
influences, description by particular characteristics like
age and sex, and by the family motifs which nurture
these socialized qualities. It is now time to introduce
the themes which cannot be so readily explained by
theories of socialization. In doing so, I concentrate on
those notions of the children which emerge forcefully or
gently in their interviews and move the children to
destinations at least partially beyond the family.

The story of socialization differences and influences,
as they manifest themselves in the children's imagery,
may give way to a script written in universal language.
Yet the children's scenario is not that simple. Socialization creates a durable transparency over these common
themes, and it is a difficult covering to unveil. In
describing each major common theme, I begin with
possible examples of socialization overlay. Yet I also
find that the seven themes seem to have a life of their

own, an existence beyond the world of family interpretations and family experience. Thus each theme seems to exist in the child's inner world at three levels:

1. *Family interpretation: Institutional religion.* Parents' and other family members' interpretations and communications of largely formal religious dogma and ritual (and occasional reference to religious teachers). Their interpretations are then projected onto the child's deity conception.
2. *Child's interpretation: Family.* The child's internal interpretation and understanding of parents, siblings, and family atmosphere. These interpretations are then also projected onto the deity representation.
3. *Child's self-awareness.* The child's own self-perception or world, independent of the child's family imagery. The self-perceptions are either projected onto the God figure or can be seen as being identical to the representation.

In embarking upon this many-layered terrain, the distinctions of Wilfred Cantwell Smith in *The Meaning and End of Religion* are well worth taking to heart: "Theology is part of the traditions, is part of this world. Faith lies beyond theology, in the hearts of men. Truth lies beyond faith, in the heart of God" (1962, 113). In forging a transition from the themes of socialized tradition to motifs of a common faith, I try to take all of us deeper into the hearts of my child interviewees. Whether or not these collective themes even begin to approach the Truth may be unanswerable; certainly it is unapproachable through the crude processes of understanding that I bring. One thing seems more certain, however. As Max Heirich concludes in "A Change of Heart" (1977), the deepest experiences that we label "spiritual" are not so easily explained by the social and situational explanations we often apply. Something beyond, whether manmade or otherwise created, clearly seems at work and at play. But it is time once again to let the children speak for themselves.

The Qualified Power of the Deity

The first of these common descriptions of God revolves around power—a sense of "more-than-human" impact on the universe. While largely unbounded, this power does not seem total and meets with qualification in the children's responses. "Why else would there be wars?" the children seem to reason, and they further imply that God's power is somehow irrevocably linked and dependent upon man. How exactly man is involved is ambiguous for the children, each child formulating a hypothesis, rationalization, or old-fashioned guess as he or she wishes.

For example, at the level of family interpretation, the children might associate power with the capacity of churches to regulate and enforce guidelines of moral conduct. Most likely, this would be a message their parents have passed on to them. As ten-year-old Annette, a Baptist child, explains, "The Church wants us to attend every Sunday. This is God's will." At the level of children's interpretation, power might emerge as a deity who offers direction and influences the growth of the child. As the Hindu group's twelve-year-old Artie calmly offers, in a way that very much makes God sound like a parent figure, "God has the power to care."

Yet beyond these two dimensions, power takes on quite a different shape, a form which I am calling "self-awareness." In these instances, power seems to be the deepest and most internalized by the child. The deity emerges as one who has "an efficacy about the stars," even if this is somehow qualified and muted by reality. The child, too, as if responding to the qualities of the deity, seems to be a proactive agent in his or her own right. As twelve-year-old Mark of the Baptist group exclaims in a conversation with his mother, "Mom, I believe we must do things ourselves too ... even though I believe God helps us." Glimpses of this type of power are what we discover in common across the forty children. Let's turn to some other examples.

Eleven-year-old Becky Sue, a Catholic child, answers the description question with a single word, "powerful." She later explains that her parents and Sunday school teacher have communicated this to her. But further along, as Becky Sue seems more relaxed with me and more candid, she inadvertantly describes some examples of power and also of the limitations of God's power. In response to the "death of an older person" query, Becky Sue spontaneously notes:

> God takes away people's suffering, like from cancer. He has the power to do that and he uses death in that way. But he must not have full control—otherwise he would cure the cancer.

Like Harold Kushner, the author of *Why Bad Things Happen to Good People* (1981), little Becky Sue apparently prefers to believe in an all-good God rather than one that is all-powerful. And like her child counterparts, she also points to human efficacy: "People have an important role in working to cure and alleviate the pain of cancer." What emerges is a picture of a benign deity who leaves room for human effort and the human heart as well.

Twelve-year-old Gerald, a representative of the Baptist group, manifests a highly different socialization background than Becky's but a similar underlying conception of the deity's power. Gerald describes God's involvement in the family scenario very much within the domain of a child's interpretation. The scenario is one of family tension. Into this conflict enters the spirit of the deity:

> He's gonna calm everything down. He has the
> power to work though Jesus to help people to love.
> ... In the end [Gerald points to the five family
> dolls], the family will find love.

We get a hint of a conception in flux, however, when
Gerald informs us at the outset of the "child alone"
scenario that "God is inside the boy." Slowly, the nature
of power changes—it changes in a way that locates
greater power in Gerald's own small hands. In reaction
to the interview section on changes, Gerald offers a
most surprising and interesting response, speaking
from the first-person point of view:

> I am going to try to make everybody love each
> other more. I am going to do this starting now. I
> feel like I can make a difference by doing the best I
> can.

Out of the midst of family tensions and a child's clear
interpretation of this turmoil, Gerald discovers new-
found power. Change is possible, he determines, and he
speaks with a sense of confidence about his own power
and the power of his deity. At this brief juncture, his
deity representation is less determined by a familial
conception, though he finds that God can be applied to
help the family.

The notion of power has been viewed as central by a
vast array of theologians and philosophers, doubters
as well as believers. The great skeptic, Friedrich
Nietzsche, saw power as the paramount quality of
nearly all manmade God conceptions. He believed that
the idea of God arose from man's struggles with his own
sense of power and powerlessness. According to
Nietzsche (1888), a deity is falsely posited to account for
these feelings. It seems the element of doubt, as well as
the relationship between divine and personal power in

the children's responses, may provide a kind of evidence for a Nietzsche-like view. Yet it is not clear that power experienced as "close to the self," such as that universally indicated by the children, necessarily has only a mundane or human origin.

Sometimes the children seem to conceive of power as a thoroughly inner emotional experience. They speak of "moving moments" that feel very powerful, like when they helped an injured, smaller child. But these special moments have some philosophical backing as well. We have already mentioned that such heightened moments, *darshan*, are emphasized in the Hindu tradition. Pascal called them *pensées*, powerful insights as something inexplicable is glimpsed (Küng 1981). I am reminded here of the words of eleven-year-old David, one of the Jewish participants, as he spoke of his feelings toward the deity:

> Sometimes I just feel a kind of overwhelmed and excited feeling about all that God has done in the world. . . . It is hard to understand but you can sort of sense the power—like when we went on a trip and saw the Grand Canyon. It was amazing.

The Intimacy of the Deity

Universally, the children depict a deity that demonstrates a capacity for intimacy—a closeness between and among human beings. They imply that the very nature of God is complexly and profoundly related to intimacy. Precisely how the divine resides in the realm of closeness, or rather, how human intimacy rests in the domain of the deity, is not entirely clear to the children.

Most often, children, their families, and their friends are the targets or providers of intimacy, which appears as emotional energy. Ordinarily, some sense of intimacy, however relative, transpires between God and child. The degree and type of intimacy may vary greatly, ranging from the children of God, the Lover, to the children of the distant God. Yet despite these vast differences, intimacy is woven subtly into the very fabric of the God design.

For example, at the level of the family's interpretation of formal religion, some children speak of intimacy as a mass congregation of likeminded practitioners and the experience of shared worship. Or the children might couch intimacy in terms of religious dogma or historical events (e.g., six-year-old Gary, a Catholic child, talks of the closeness between Jesus and his disciples). At the level of the children's interpretation of family, intimacy appears in its many conventional uses. Frequently, as with many of the Catholic children, God is involved in keeping the family emotionally close and implicitly takes part in furthering kinship ties to others. In contrast to these more institutional forms, the children also suggest an intimacy more focused on themselves. It has the character of an "in-touchness" with themselves, usually surfacing in regard to quiet contemplation or self-initiated prayer. The deity is then associated with the aspects of the self that are discovered at such times.

Eight-year-old Dan of the Catholic group demonstrates a strong tendency toward institutionally based intimacy, though something more original also seems emergent. In discussion following his story, Dan volunteers that he would "like to have broken bread with Jesus . . . and been a part of the things Jesus did with the disciples." Here, symbolic food and ritualism appear in an atmosphere of comraderie. Dan conveys a desire to be close to the origins and originators of his religious group. Yet a more spontaneous sense of intimacy appears in Dan's response to the question about God's everyday activities:

God can do things with you, in a way. Like, God is

with you when you draw or write a story. . . . He is
always there when you're trying to make something or do something on your own.

As Dan implies, his God is an intimate part of his
personal world of creativity and self-expression. The
closeness of God and child is reminiscent of the relationship between artistic inspiration and artist. God seems
to exist as the wellspring of ideas and emotions at Dan's
creative core.

Eight-year-old Miriam of the Jewish group makes
frequent mention of intimacy with some references that
are institutionally oriented and with others that are
self-oriented. In her drawing and story, she depicts the
trials and tribulations of the Jewish people and explains
that these ordeals are tempered by the close bond that
the people shared. In play scenarios, Miriam describes a
similar closeness among the family dolls. She transforms the miniature boy and girl into the "Jewish
Bobsey twins"—an indication of their inseparability
and propinquity. Later, however, Miriam's tone grows
more serious as she discusses her wish "to live close to
her idea of a rich life." She says she feels good when she
lives like this, because this life style is closer to God.
Asked what such a rich life style would be like, Miriam
answers with allusions to both formal religious imagery
(e.g., "close to Truth," the Old Testament scroll) and
apparently more original imagery: "I feel rich when I
feel happy about myself . . . and staying with what I
really believe."

One of the most interesting characteristics of the
intimacy theme is the apparent relationship between
intimacy and faith or doubt in the deity. All the children
show a marked tendency to associate intimacy with
episodes of faith and the lack of intimacy with episodes
of doubt. As mentioned previously, twelve-year-old
Artie of the Hindu group talks of enjoying a closeness

with Baba and "of feeling very spiritual at these times."
Alternatively, Artie refers to people who have doubt
about Baba and then quickly dissociates himself from
these people in terms of intimacy: "I do not feel close to
these people." Furthermore, in responding to the "famous figures" portion of the interview, Artie again
stresses intimacy and its relation to faith:

> Ghandi and God are different in that Ghandi was a
> person, though he was a person who was knowl-
> edgeable about the ways of God. . . . Ghandi was
> close to God because he had a great deal of faith—
> his faith allowed him to accomplish many changes.

Thus the articulate Artie, like the other children despite their diverse religious backgrounds, voices the
belief that intimacy and self-awareness bring one closer
to a deity, or at least, to one's inner conception and faith
in a God.

In philosophy and literature, the importance of intimacy in God representations usually appears in the
form of personal, experiential encounters. René
Descartes, for example, resolved "not to seek after any
science" to pursue the divine but "to seek what might be
in myself" (1644). William James, in tracing the nature of man's stream of consciousness, asserted that
spiritual meaning and truth are to be found in our
present experiences. James conceived of God as a reality
close to us within that experience (Vanden Burgt 1981).

Omnipresence

The forty children, despite their sometimes glaring
socialization differences, share the underlying belief
that the deity knows no physical or lawful limitations.
It exists in all time and space. It is ubiquitous. Even the
eldest group of children, who often struggle with the
issue of limitations, infer that God is ultimately beyond
constraint.

While each child presents some sense of an omnipresent God, the particular description of ubiquity differs from child to child. For some children, and the youngest interviewees in particular, this presence means physical proximity. For others, omnipresence speaks to a spirit in the air which is always there in potential, if only people were open to its existence. For still other children, omnipresence has a more self-focused meaning as it indicates a certainty about an accessible God.

At the level of the family's interpretation, omnipresence may appear in the form of the everpresent formal religion or repetitive ritual. At the level of the child's interpretation, omnipresence might indicate a sense of always being with the family no matter what the course of events. This presence can be experienced by a child as literal or figurative. Literally, it indicates physical proximity to members of the nuclear family. More often, however, a figurative interpretation means that a child "carries family members and family feeling inside." Finally, in terms of a child's appreciation of himself or herself, omnipresence frequently suggests a great reliability and consistency of mood and behavior. Phenomenologically, the child feels as if the same "self" is always there.

Four-year-old Barbie of the Hindu group provides a brief description of a child who is preoccupied with the institutional layers of omnipresence. Her most memorable comment was, "God is always here. God is always walking in my mind." Because of a ready parroting of her mother's understanding of formal religion, Barbie seems to have internalized a rather intrusive parent figure that, under the flagship of the deity, treads not so softly in her mind. As Barbie speaks, she seems to also be conveying something about the emerging presence of her conscience—soon to be fully formed. Yet, for Barbie, omnipresence seems to have a slightly perjorative and highly socialized meaning, even if she occasionally approaches greater originality.

Sandra, an eight-year-old Jewish child, also presents several layers of understanding, yet she provides more evidence of a conception that is perhaps beyond socialization. Sandra's "family interpretation" layer is evident as she responds to the naming task. To name the deity, she constructs an amalgam of Hebrew and English:

> I call it *Hashem.* But in English, I think of it as like everything and everywhere. Sometimes we call it everything and everywhere.

Sandra continues to explain that she learned this from her teachers and from her parents. She provides a rendition of her father's explanation: "He often says, 'God is everywhere and appears everywhere in the Old Testament—with the Jews in Egypt, on Mount Sinai, and when they reach the Promised Land, too.' " In contrast to these more obviously socialized memories, Sandra episodically reverts to a different, more singular voice, as in her description of the deity:

> I feel a kind of presence always with me. It kind of gives me peace . . . makes me feel good . . . knowing that it is always there even if I can't see it or feel it.

Sandra's words speak to the positive feelings that most of the children seem to experience concerning this omnipresence. They frequently suggest a certain tranquility, if also a certain ineffability and wonderment concerning more spontaneous experiences of omnipresence.

Cross-culturally and cross-historically, omnipresence has been cited as an important characteristic of deity conceptions. The omnipresence of a deity was, in fact, a central understanding in Chinese civilization at the time of the Chou dynasty, from 1111–249 B.C. (Küng 1981). In contemporary writing, *The Joyful Community* of Benjamin Zablocki highlights an ever-ready and everpresent holy spirit in the belief system of the German Bruderhof commune (Zablocki 1971). In noting similar conceptions from diverse eras and places, Stace (1952) emphasized the importance of time and eternity in these conceptions. Clearly, the time-honored representation is of a God that transcends time and spans eternity.

Interestingly, Descartes spoke of omnipresence in the same breath with the self and with a sense of certainty. He saw the everpresent God as "the epochal turning point," the point at which the existence of the deity validates the certainty of the self (1644). The close relationship between the omnipresent deity conception and the self is echoed in the common responses of the children as well.

Anxiety in Relation to the Deity

Throughout the children's responses, an unusual amount of anxiety is obvious surrounding the image of God—a tension that far surpasses what we might expect from children facing an unfamiliar interviewer. The pervasive anxiety seems highly related to specific deity content rather than performance concerns alone. Anxiety appears especially prevalent when a child attempts to make a firm, declarative statement about a deity. As the child tries to express a spontaneous belief in the midst of the world's considerable ambiguity and doubt, anxiety is at the forefront of consciousness.

The anxiety manifested consistently by the children also seems foreign to the tension-filled artifacts of cognitive difficulties and misunderstandings. When the children struggle with cognitive limitations, as sometimes occurs with the younger children, their anxiety has a different quality. Such anxiety is associated with the experience of immediate frustration and the fear of inadequacy. It seems to dissipate when the child feels reassured or proceeds to a concept he or she understands. The God-related anxiety does not have these qualities and does not seem to diminish as the child speaks more confidently.

Examples of anxiety at various levels of socialization are easily discernible. At the level of family interpretation, the children manifest frequent anxiety concerning obedience to codes of moral conduct and adherence to religious stricture (e.g., Mark, age twelve, of the Baptist group, who speaks so nervously). At the layer of the child's interpretation of family, anxiety may reflect myriad causes, including typical family dynamics. However, as anxiety seems to transcend these family influences, it appears in relation to deep consideration of the self and of the mysteries of the world. Such anxiety is not as easily explained by family concerns and unconscious family dynamics alone.

Before proceeding to examples from the children, it may be helpful to elucidate further the nature of this deity-related anxiety. As the anxiety is exhibited by the children, it seems to possess a quality of powerful attraction as well as powerful resistance. It seems as if the children are drawn tremendously to their deity conceptions, a symbol and pinnacle of yearnings. Yet they are equally fearful. The result is this great anxiety, which causes the children to go in a variety of directions. Some may wish to move away from the anxiety and its exploration when it appears. Others, perhaps those whose personalities allow greater anxiety tolerance, demonstrate a dedicated persistence in trying to unravel some of their own confusions and the ambiguities of their God representations.

Nine-year-old Arthur's socialized anxiety surfaces early, as he relates the names "Lord" and "God" with a reverent anxiety and brief tremor that seemed to suggest a solemn Baptist training. Yet, surprisingly, Arthur displays a different sort of anxiety at times of more difficult self-expression. When confronted with the difficult question about God's role in the death of a young person, Arthur hesitated and then, as if fighting with his reluctance, presented an interesting response. It seemed as if he had chosen to struggle with his anxiety:

> It must be a complicated God. It's often hard to make sense of . . . [pause, then said with caution,] Sometimes, when I try to think about death in the world and God, I can't even stay thinking about it [pained expression].

In this moment, Arthur seemed to be experiencing a certain dread at the mystery and possible terror of the world. At the same time, he confronts his own personal doubt, at least as long as he can tolerate doubt. In fact, his subsequent responses to the belief questions, which seem to invite highly personalized statements, represent a retreat to more rote, institutionalized, and less anxiety-oriented answers.

Seven-year-old Hallie of the Jewish group is highly influenced by her own interpretations of family, resulting in some anxiety. But she also speaks about the deity with an apprehension that goes beyond interpersonal anxiety. Hallie's interview shows a fairly typical set of family dynamics, with some visible anxiety around closeness with male figures and discernible concern about other females. Her description of male authority figures in play scenarios is extensively more positive than that of female characters, and the resulting anxiety surrounding this oedipal configuration is clear. While it does socialize her God conception in predictable ways, it does not thoroughly dominate her responses. Even within this framework of interpersonal anxiety, episodes of a more nonneurotic anxiety surface, for example, in her response to the query about her feelings about the deity:

> Sometimes my feelings about God seem scary ... I feel like they're alot, but different than I feel toward people. It's hard to feel about something you don't know for sure.

Like other children of her age, Hallie uses words like "scary" or "alot" to convey her anxiety. What was most striking about Hallie's response was the sincere, centered manner in which she spoke, in contrast to her more happy-go-lucky, if not scattered, demeanor during most of the interview.

Concerning the subject of religious anxiety, William James discussed the frequent turning away from spirituality because of anxiety. James attributed this anxiety to a remarkable ineffability of the deity, as well as to man's certain speechlessness about the self. He wrote of the anxiety and how it seemed, in his view, a necessary part of the path toward a deity:

> [In regard to approaching God], one must have musical ears to know the value of a symphony; one must have been in love oneself to understand a lover's state of mind. Lacking the heart or ear, we cannot interpret the musician or the lover justly. (Vanden Burgt 1981, 127)

In *The Idea of the Holy* (1923), Rudolph Otto described how the religious dimension could not be expressed in terms of a secular set of events. Otto maintained that we could not assume to truly know human anxiety, or human nature for that matter, until we came to know the religious dimension. Like James, Otto was entirely pessimistic about our capacity to enter the religious, just as discriminating and cautious about man's attempts to describe and define the spiritual realm (Bertocci 1971).

Transformations Caused by the Deity

The deity representations of the children are invariably associated with psychological, biological, and religious transformations. Throughout their protocols, the children demonstrate a ready awareness of changes within their persons and attribute these in various ways to their deity. It is not that the children form identical attributions; some place great responsibility on the deity, others less. But all the children present the theme of transformation and wonder about the role of their God in these changes.

"Am I growing because God loves me?" a child might ask. "How can I change from being sad," another might lament. Or, "Does God have something to do with these changes I feel inside me?" All are popular questions as the children struggle with the existence and the role of God. Just as they make observations of their own changing state, the children seek to understand the changing tide of events. Their explanations range from the most mundane accounts to stirring renditions of miracles. It is along with the theme of transformations, in particular, that God representations seem so closely tied to the child's own development.

At the level of family interpretation of formal practice, transformation may assume the form of religious rites of passage—like bar mitzvah, communion, and baptism. At the level of the child's interpretation of family life, transformations grow far more complex and suggest a variety of structural and psychological circumstances—family movements, family transitions (e.g., mother returns to work), and, of course, psychosocial and internal changes in the child. Yet a transformation of the self goes beyond simple family changes and developmental processes. In this context, the children seem to refer to transformations that build on development but involve a change in world view that is, in their eyes, unusually radical. Such transformations are associated with God, even if a change in the child's perception of that God is also indicated.

Carin, the nine-year-old Catholic child highlighted in chapter 6, best portrays the theme of transformations on all three levels. Carin comfortably discusses changes indicated by her formal religious background. Among the images in Carin's protocol are the following: a person receiving a halo in a family scenario, a description of baptism in another script, and an allusion to entrance into heaven in response to the question about what she might like to ask God. Concurrently, Carin's understanding of family is also replete with references to change. For example, in reacting to the inquiry about her views versus her parents', Carin was quick to point out that her conception has recently been changing, "become older," and "become more like my parents' ideas." Interspersed between references to such conven-tional changes, Carin's responses indicate a sense of transformation that seems deeper and more wholly her own. Like the older children in the study, she shows glimpses of a more spontaneous notion of transformations.

Carin's interview stands out precisely because of such a transformation. In response to the "feelings" segment, Carin began to cry as she spoke: "I love God so much it is hard to express." At this point, Carin seemed transformed before my eyes from a young child infatuated with fantasy imagery to a young woman with deeper and more lasting feelings. Her succeeding responses and manner bear this out. While previously it had been difficult for Carin to acknowledge negative sentiments, she was finally able to voice some anger at disappointments at school. She wondered why God didn't help more, but accepted some of the responsibility herself. While Carin could not sustain this more explicit manner, her wish for a continued transformation resurfaced in her question to God: "What does it take to be a real angel?" I suspect this was a very important question for her.

Carin's plaintive question brings together her interest in transformations at all levels. Her reference to an angel speaks to an institutional influence, as well as perhaps a desire to be her father's "real angel"—a transformation on the family level. Yet the underlying motivation for the question seemed to follow from Carin's crying, and for a desire for a change in her conception of herself.

The importance of transformations in the life of the individual has been a source of fascination in psychological, philosophical, and theological circles. For example, Allport (1955) felt that psychological transformations of all types are driven by an appetite for meaning. Their form at the surface will show vast individual differences but their underlying motive force will not. This is perhaps what Sartre intended when he said, "Man transforms himself . . . I am my freedom" (1948). Sartre saw such transformations as close to the self, but he saw no necessary reason why they must be God-oriented in nature. In other words, man's meaning may be a result of man's own creation.

With regard to the study of God representations in particular, Charles Steward (1967) found that transformations are particularly striking in the imagery of children during adolescence, when family and developmental influences are clearly at the forefront. Indeed, Steward hypothesized that the God concept itself would undergo the greatest transformations during this period of the life cycle.

In view of the many others that have offered their perspectives on psychological transformations, I think James Fowler best expresses the phenomenon that the children seem to illustrate:

There are precursors of faith as attitude and

motive in the child's developmental history. However, these undergo a transformation—an enlargement, even a radical transmutation—as they are related to Ultimate Reality. (1981, 303)

Connectedness

As one of the more implicit themes among the children, and yet as one of the more recurrent even within the individual child, connectedness seems to suggest two things. First, the child believes that the world and its events all share a relationship. Second, the child seeks his or her deity as the core of this total interrelationship. One reason for the subtle nature of this motif is that its fuller appearance seems to require passing through tremendous anxiety. Despite its latent nature in the protocols, a sense of connectedness appears elemental as it brings a child closer to relationships with other people and with his or her deity.

A frequent application of connectedness at the level of family interpretation of institutions occurs in relation to religious group unity. We saw this inclination most graphically with the Hindu children, who demonstrate a sense of unity and cohesion with other ashram members in unparalleled fashion. Institutional unity is also evident in individual children, like five-year-old Harold, who emphasized that "being Jewish" made him feel part of something important. Family unity in the interpretive purview of the child might be more atmospheric, as it captures a special kinship in the family system. Yet a sense of connectedness also seems more abstract if not elusive. In the realm of the self, connectedness suggests a life in which all aspects seem to flow together for a common purpose. While it is certainly possible for this to appear without mention of a deity, the children seem to relate its expression to their God.

Numerous children provide examples of the socialized layers of connectedness. With regard to the institution of formal religion, the following individual examples accompany the Hindu group's collective illustration: twelve-year-old Mark of the Baptist group notes that he "gets a high out of being together in church with everyone"; nine-year-old Ted comments that being a Catholic "makes you feel a kind of spirit with other Catholics"; six-year-old Aaron colorfully adds that "going to the ashram is wild because everyone chants together." Similar enthusiasm is voiced in regard to a sense of family unity. Eight-year-old Sandra of the Jewish group describes "a warm, happy feeling" with her family around the Friday dinner table; ten-year-old Lenny of the Catholic group emphasizes that "seeing all of his family at Christmastime makes him realize what is important."

Among all these children, twelve-year-old Tamara is unusually thoughtful as she illustrates a more spontaneous sense of connectedness. Her various responses capture the types of implicit images of other children concerning a universal connectedness. In the "parents alone" scenario, her doll parents are not concerned with everyday worries or differences between them. Instead, "they feel good about life and feel a part of mankind in a good way" (connectedness of people). Notice that Tamara does not deny that trivial differences may exist, but she subordinates these to a greater sense of affinity. In the "child alone" scenario, the little girl doll cries out "past pain" and "feels closer to God, as her pain turns into joy" (connectedness, as well as transformation, of emotions). Finally, in responding to the death questions, she offers perhaps a more basic image: "It is all woven together . . . everyone's lives. . . . And God is at the center." With this notion of the connectedness of man and God, Tamara illustrates that connectedness and even interconnectedness are significant for her in a most conscious way, perhaps brought to the surface by her group affiliation. Yet however more quietly and intricately expressed, the theme of connectedness is exceptionally constant in all forty child interviewees.

Connectedness as a motif has received its share of criticism as well as descriptions of discovery and support. Nietzsche comments, "Man deludes himself when he assumes a totality, a systemization, indeed any organization in all events" (1888, 221). In contrast, Socrates maintained that such "unity" was one of the basic forms of the universe. Plato adopted this theme and elaborated on its meaning. According to Paul Shorey, Plato stands out because he believed there was a perfectability in which all thoughts, words, and acts met (Shorey 1903).

Interest in the theme of connectedness has continued throughout the centuries from a variety of sources. Saint Augustine was perhaps the first to apply this unity to bodies of knowledge, implying the complete synthesis of apparently opposite spheres like faith and reason. Following the Middle Ages, Descartes and Pascal used different languages to convey a similar notion (Küng 1981). Among more contemporary philosophers, Martin Buber has added that this unification is never final in the eyes of man, and it is incumbent upon man to seek its fulfillment (Lefevre 1963).

The cross-cultural reliability of this theme is most noteworthy, for it occupies perhaps an even more exalted place in non-Western belief systems. In *Childhood and Cosmos* (1973), Pierre Erny elegantly makes this very point about African cultures and the prevailing philosophy behind their child rearing. While Erny suggests that socialization is part of the basis for this sense of unity, he asserts a more mysterious and religious explanation:

The African cosmos is like a spider web: its least element cannot be touched without making the whole vibrate. Everything is connected, interdependent. Everything cooperates to make a unity. Nevertheless, man occupies a special place in this universe. (1973, 19)

Against the backdrop of these more "heavy sounding" notions of interconnectedness, children seem to occupy a special place in the universe of philosophers. We conclude the theme of connectedness with the insightful words of the main character in *Mister God, This Is Anna*. Little Anna concludes upon reflection, "We're all playing the same chord to Mister God but with different names" (Fynn 1974, 97).

The Theme of Light

Light is perhaps the most intangible of the themes and the most difficult to articulate. It is also the most surprising to this interviewer, as it stands virtually outside of my own everyday construct system. Yet like a small lamp only barely visible through the darkness of the child's bedroom, light emerges through the children's responses in a variety of ways.

In the world of the child, light may appear as an accoutrement of the deity itself, or as a symbol of its presence. Light also may be revealed as a means of communication between God and man, a spiritual messenger delivering a divine message. Occasionally, usually by implication or metaphor, light appears in the children's responses as a characteristic related to the child himself or herself, closely associated with the child's self-image.

At the institutional level of family interpretation, light frequently surfaces in the form of biblical references (e.g., the words "Let there be light" and ritual candle lighting). At the level of family life, light may be the focus of these religious observances in which the family is involved. But light in reference to the self is ordinarily more figurative. It may speak to an inner, ineffable quality, "a glow in the self." Several children use this or similar expressions for an attempt to describe the phenomenon of light.

Samples from the children speak to the influence of formal religion and family interpretation on the motif of light. Representing the Catholic religion, nine-year-old Carol relates her story and merges the biblical story of Jesus' birth, the healing works of Jesus, and her own creative additions. In explaining how healing takes place, Carol describes,

> And he probably looks up in the stars, and the
> stars bring light on that person that has a problem
> ... It brings light in it and that's how it heals the
> person.

Here, Carol uses "light" to indicate what is transferred from the divine to man. She also illustrates her own cleverness by employing a play on words—Jesus "brings light" on the problem. Not only has Carol adopted some conventional religious imagery, but she has also been influenced by its secular, colloquial uses as well.

Eight-year-old Dina, a Baptist child, presents a view of light that is largely dictated by her internalization of family concerns. Humorously, in responding to the "where does God live" question, Dina attempts to differentiate God's habitat from human homes: "Well, God's home doesn't have lights and stuff." Earlier, in a more typical example, Dina includes light as a symbol for sexuality, excitement, and inconsistency. In a family scenario, the father doll is involved in turning the lights on and off and this sets the children off in frenetic play. Here Dina relates light to the "electric feeling" she gets around her father.

But light has a different and less apparently socialized connotation for some children, such as nine-year-old Ted of the Catholic group. Light surfaces initially in institutionalized and stereotyped form, as in the conspicuous halo of light in Ted's drawing. Yet the nature of the light theme changes as Ted's interview progresses. In discussing his feelings about the deity, Ted describes a "warm, glowing feeling ... a feeling that helps you feel good about yourself." Ted further explains upon inquiry,

> I don't know what to call it exactly, but it's sort of like there's a little light inside you ... Even when something goes wrong, like when my sister died, it still can shine. I can't say I feel this all the time— but when I feel it I feel it very strong [look of enchantment].

This is the nature of how light manifests itself in the children's protocols. Interestingly, in addition to providing the most lucid description of the light theme, Ted was the only child never to use a gender-related pronoun for the deity, and he thus provided a deity conception of minimal anthropomorphism.

The notion of light as a spiritual idea is succinctly expressed by Martin Buber: "When an individual has a total relationship with another, a Thou relation, this has a light of its own and all else lives in its light" (Lefevre 1973, 35).

Writing in the transpersonal psychology literature, Richard Mann (1984) emphasizes the importance of light in Eastern thought and in his own observations on Western thought. He discusses light as a virtually universal symbol of the absolute, and suggests a path of spiritual development in regard to light: an individual moves from the venue of "there is the light" to the culminating perspective of "I am the light."

In a most intriguing argument in *The Reflexive Universe* (1976), scientist and inventor Arthur Young offers a confirming statement on the centrality of light in the physical universe. Young's perspective seems remarkably consonant with the implicit theme suggested by the children. Basing his argument on theoretical quantum physics, Young finds that light is a primary and purposive entity. It is, according to Young, not just another particle but the base element of all things. He maintains that light is not limited by time or lawful constraints. Thus, in language appropriate for an investigation of religious imagery, Young upholds the "ultimate centrality or primacy of light as the origin of everything" (1976, 34). This seems a fitting and thought-provoking comment on which to conclude the seventh of the children's common themes.

Epilogue: Common Themes

The major common themes present an array of motifs which may not easily be explained by socialization or developmental change, both of which would promise greater differences among the forty children. Whether the children are tapping into something uniquely spiritual or merely expressing something universal but rationally explainable is left for the individual observer to decide. One thing is certain. It is paradoxical that the themes that bring the children closest to themselves as individuals also bring them together through the God conception they have in common.

9

Conclusion: Implications for Childhood Religion

Dear God,
When is the best time I can talk with you?
I know you are always listening, but when
will you be listening especially hard in Ann
Arbor, Michigan?

Sincerely Yours,
Allen

In writing of children's stories, author C. S. Lewis advocates that a child spontaneously discover his or her own spiritual meanings. "Children are at least as wise [as we are] in the moral sphere," Lewis quips. It is in this spirit that I interviewed forty unique children and have attempted to describe their conceptions of God.

As the chapters have unfolded, I have traced the children's thematic representations by socialization grouping and suggested several prominent familial themes which help to account for these socialized representations. In highlighting the common themes of the children, I have observed how layers of socialization of the deity representation, however deep, are transcended by more original expressions. I believe that such original responses are very much within the spirit of moral spontaneity that C. S. Lewis spoke of. But given that there seems to be a conflict between institutional imagery and spontaneous imagery for the children, what implications does this offer for individual parents?

This question seems to me to be most crucial, a

consideration which deserves our full attention. To begin to address these additional implications, I am dividing our discussion into two portions: (1) the implications for parents concerning children's view of institutional religion; and (2) the implications for parents concerning children's view of family. To truly address these concerns, I return to the words of the children themselves, who, as Lewis suggests, are as informative as any author or storyteller.

Implications for Parents: Socialization by Institution

A major part of the socialization of a God representation is the influence of formal religion on the child. Ordinarily transmitted through the family and, to a lesser extent, through teachers and through reading, religious dogma, ritual, and lore emerge time and time again in the children's interview productions. Parents, who are after all the major communicators and interpreters of established religion, will be particularly interested in learning of the outstanding trends in relation to institutional religion that the child interviewees display. Thus the thematic trends that are outlined below are presented in the spirit of "what parents should know about their children's views of institutional religion."

Initial Positive View

On the whole, the children first indicate some positive investment in their respective religious heritages. They show eagerness to learn about biblical and historical characters and seem to take pleasure in the magic of religious rituals.

Examples from various children are typified by five-year-old Harold of the Jewish group. In reference to the numerous holidays in the Jewish religion, Harold sim-

ply comments, "Being Jewish can be fun." Children
representing other religious groups express similar
sentiment in their own ways, though older children are
already beginning to qualify their responses. Eight-
year-old Dina thinks that "getting dressed up for
church feels good," but she parenthetically adds, "not
so much when it's hot." (Her drawing of a "dressed-up"
God appears below.) Meanwhile, the Hindu group's
twelve-year-old Artie tells me that "chanting gives us a
good feeling," but later questions the sincerity of some
group members.

Constraint by Formal Religion

Such positive associations to ritual and dogma begin to
be overshadowed by reservation and discontent, however. A significant portion of the children's conceptions
seems dictated and constrained by established conceptions, particularly as children are introduced to orthodox representations by family and teachers. Inevitably,
the religious institution assumes a parental role in the
child's mind.

In the description division of the interview, Annette,
the ten-year-old Baptist group participant, begins not
with an original response but with an echo of her
Sunday school teacher, albeit with mixed feelings that
lead her to stammer:

> Well in, um, Sunday school, in Sunday school . . .
> My Sunday school teacher said that Jesus had a
> cloth pulled around him . . . I think my mother told
> me that too . . . So I guess that's what God looks
> like . . .

Following this response, Annette sought to "test out"
how I would react to a more original view. When she
sensed that I would not be critical, she proceeded with
caution to open up. It seemed a major personal triumph
when she was able to speak in a first-person voice. She

Drawing by eight-year-old Dina

said, very softly, "Well, when I pray to God when I'm all by myself, I feel happiness . . . like I'm really talking to him." It seemed to me that at such rare times Annette also felt like she was really being herself.

Interference by Formal Religion

As Annette infers with her response, formal religion and adults' interpretation frequently act as go-betweens for the child and deity conception. Sometimes, they are unwelcome interferences at that. There is a recurrent sense throughout the children's protocols that they desire a more direct encounter or experience with their God. They seem to feel that such encounters are forbidden; they also harbor much trepidation about foregoing the intercession of adults.

In reaction to the "communication with the deity" inquiries, nine-year-old Carol, also of the Baptist group, says that she does not talk "straight away" to God. "Other people who are older," Carol adds with emphasis, "may be in touch with God themselves." Here, Carol makes a cryptic reference to her parents, who in her eyes act as if they speak directly to God. She is not granted this privilege, and this prescribed indirectness corresponds to an interpersonal indirectness that she demonstrates elsewhere in her protocol. Formal religion, as interpreted by the adults in Carol's life, seems to leave her with a reluctance about direct and spontaneous relating—at least in regard to matters of world view and matters of consequence.

Disenchantment with Routine

One of the primary difficulties children experience with formal religion, or with its communication through their families, is the tendency for obsessive routine to be encouraged. In other words, the children see formal religious practice as dry and obligatory. In the most typical scenario, church, synagogue or ashram became the enforcing symbol of unpopular religious routine.

In his family scenario, eleven-year-old Sean of the Catholic group explains,

> The family is eating Sunday dinner and God comes down and says: "Did you go to Mass this morning?" God gets mad and wonders why they didn't. So, the next Sunday they all go to Mass. They decide to go to Mass each week.

Sean's words speak to the great extent to which the children associate religion with obedience. Sometimes, as Sean indicates, the children see religious practice as thoroughly out of their control. They occasionally appear as the small marionettes of religious theater, acting and revealing a prepared script.

The children differ greatly in how much resentment they manifest in reaction to perceived religious control. Sean's strivings are perhaps more dampened than most, and so is any visible discontent that he might feel. Other children convey a sense of tension with the practice of formal rituals, but usually a degree of unhappiness seems acceptable within the frameworks of their religions and within their home environment. The primary tension-filled concerns of the majority children may be summarized as follows:

1. Excessive emphasis by religious group and pare on religious worship attendance rather than qua of belief (e.g, "I wish my family would talk n about what we believe"—nine-year-old Carol).
2. Inordinate concern with expectations of ot rather than one's own expectations with rega religion (e.g., "It's hard for me to say what lieve"—six-year-old Gary).
3. Concern with the letter and propriety of rather than the spirit in which ritual is per (e.g., "We light candles on Fridays, but I don' understand why"—seven-year-old Hallie).
4. Intrusive orientation toward a good/bad

which seems to result in too "conscience-oriented" a religious practice (e.g., the four- to six-year-old children, who are the most graphic in this regard).

5. Last, and most universal, the tendency of formal religious teachers and parents to block noninstitutional or unconventional views, and thus to discourage original belief and discovery (e.g., "I wish my Sunday school teacher would let us draw"—five-year-old Harold).

Socialization Effects of Other Institutions

In addition to the pronounced influence of formal religion and its interpretation, the children indicate several other institutions which have a secondary impact on their deity conceptions. While somewhat filtered by parents and other adults, these other institutions are relatively independent, more frequently associated with school and the educational system. They include science and technology and media and television.

Science and technology sometimes seem to act as a monolithic competitor to formal religion; at other times science and technology act as contributors to already-existing formal conceptions. Science and technology harness great manmade power in the eyes of the child, as they appear to make little in life impossible or unexplainable. Together with formal religion, science and technology stand as pillars of socialization which can dominate the individual child in their enormity.

In no child's protocol was a scientific imprint more evident than in that of eight-year-old Nellie of the Jewish group, whose unusual drawing appears below. As she explains in her story, Nellie intends to depict a magnifying glass by which we can see the molecules that make up God. One of only two children to draw no human form, Nellie describes her deity with much science-oriented detail. Later she suggests that "God's home may be around Saturn somewhere" and then

Drawing by eight-year-old Nellie

alludes to the modern-day, scientific proof for the existence of Noah's Ark.

At the same time, Nellie quotes scripture, implying
that religion and science, woven together, determine

her world view. Both are highly influential and she sees no necessary discrepancy. For Nellie, the tension appears, not in regard to religion versus science, but in relation to these institutional views versus the development of her own personal view. She is terribly apprehensive about voicing any disagreement with science or with religion, though we gain brief glimpses of her desire for more spontaneous expression. For example, she cautiously asks, "Can I use my favorite color to draw?" Thus Nellie, along with other children, implies that scientific and technological imagery work their way into deity representations and frequently inhibit personal discovery.

Another institutional origin of deity content is television and the media, which present countless illustrations of gods and superhero characters. The forms of popular literature, movies, and television are clearly pronounced in the children's protocols. These socializing forms colorfully shape the children's heroic ideals and fantasy constructions. Much national attention has been payed to the effects of media exposure on children's aggression, but little has been noted concerning media influences on religious development. Yet undoubtedly for my forty interviewees, media conceptions of God and media figures are no less important than formal religion and scientific conceptions.

Among other examples, ten-year-old Scott of the Baptist group sets a scene of God versus evil forces in his story and identifies the deity with the "good guy stars" of "Starsky and Hutch," the television crime-fighting series. Later in the interview, Scott comments that conversations with God can be quite unusual, "like when God talked to Moses through a burning bush in [the movie] *The Ten Commandments*." Fictitious media conceptions also can be employed as a point of similarity or contrast to formal religious conceptions, and thus can play a role in doubt and religious tension. As Scott pungently offers, "God might be just as unreal as Hercules or one of the Greek gods in the movies."

What Scott exemplifies is a media-dominated conception, one which emerges in less blatant fashion among other children. The children periodically demonstrate a reliance on a television or media representation of a deity rather than a formal religious or personal conception. Given the emphasis in the media on pictorial representations, children who are heavily media-influenced report very anthropomorphic images. They describe familiar and human gods who may co-star with Charleton Heston or may make a guest appearance on a crime-fighter show. Particularly when anxious or confused, the children seem to rely on popular depictions of God because these notions are accessible and involve little personal risk to espouse. Their deities are perhaps "Madison Avenue" versions of God, the result of secular socialization which may comply with or diverge from orthodox religious versions.

The children differ markedly as to whether they express dissonance in regard to such media conceptions, that is, in how much they believe in or discount these incarnations. Yet one commonality does stand out among the children—the popular media stereotypes do impede the child's own spiritual explorations in much the same way that they might obstruct children's imaginative processes. While the more independent-minded children will proceed with their own creations and beliefs nonetheless, they do so by traveling with trepidation against the tide of popular views.

Striving for Personal Expression

Struggling against this excessive socialization, the children tell us that the picture needs to be completed. They communicate a great striving for deity-related exploration and a great yearning for more expansive personal experience and belief. During the drawing, story, and scenario segments of interviews, the children express both reservation and budding excitement about expressing their own ideas about God.

Illustrations of the desire for open expression abound among the children. It is, in fact, difficult to do justice to their abundance without presenting all the interviews. But a few examples should capture the children's general orientation:

1. Seven-year-old Hallie (after telling the biblical story of Joseph): "Now, can I tell one of my own?"
2. Six-year-old Gary (during the family scenario): "Is it okay if I don't have them in church praying?"
3. Seven-year-old Jeri (spontaneous comment as interview ends): "Can I say some things about God I thought up myself?"
4. Six-year-old Jan (spontaneous comment as interview concludes): "Can I draw another picture different from the first [a solemn portrait of a rabbilike figure]? I'd like to draw some flowers that God made."
5. Nine-year-old Ted (responding to the "changes" question, as he looks up inquisitively at me): "If I could really ask him anything I want, I would ask God why he doesn't change the taste of spinach."

These are the voices of children who search for a certain spiritual and expressive freedom. Their creativity, poignancy, and humor stand out as religious views in their own right. They seem to be asking for a free atmosphere to discover what the nature of God might be.

Thus, in regard to the institutions of formal religion and its interpretation and other institutions which portray religious conceptions, children indicate a common conflict: the representations of institutional teaching versus the quest for discovery of personal representations. In their desire for more spontaneous and open expression, the children seem to be saying about this conflict what has been eloquently said of an adult's religious beliefs: "A person's faith is essentially his own and is in principle beyond external domination" (Smith 1962, 67).

Implications for Parents: Socialization by Family

Not only does the family act as the ultimate interpreter of most institutional teachings and popular conceptions, but it profoundly shapes the child's interpersonal view of the world. While familial images may vary across individual children, as we saw in chapter 7, some of the determinants of the permanence of familial imprints do not.

In collecting the imagery of these forty children, I find over and over that certain determinants will consistently affect a child's capacity for deity-related expression. These determinants seem to form something of a pattern—a pathway of spiritual development that takes a child from a more parental and socialized conception to a more self-initiated representation of a personal God. I present these critical determinants, and imply that their sequential relationship presents a pattern of child development, with the pragmatics of child care in mind. Thus, once again, discussion is inspired by the basic question, "What should parents know about their children's views of family-related religion?"

The Paramount Importance of Trust

There are many parenting characteristics that are probably vital in spiritually rich caretaking, the type of child rearing that allows a child to explore the mysteries of the universe. Among such qualities are the following: tolerance, optimism, limit-setting, and a zest for originality and novelty. Yet perhaps no phenomenon is as necessary and as sufficient in parenting as the establishment of trust.

In speaking here of trust, we mean to include the basic trust of the early mother/child relationship. In addition, we also refer to the continuing trust that parents can nurture in a child through steady and sensitive attention. The combination of these forms of trust, one form building naturally on the other, represents a prime precursor to faith in God—any God. Trust is not necessarily the first cause of that faith, owing to the possibility that faith may be caused by the actual existence of a deity; but trust is the process which makes it possible for faith to emerge in the child. By laying the groundwork for stable representations, trust permits a deity representation to have consistent meaning in the child's inner world.

One trend is quite clear among the forty children. Those youngsters who evidence healthier and more secure parental relations evidence more positive deity conceptions, though emotional investment in the God figure does not turn on health alone. Let's look to some examples from the children's interviews.

David, an eleven-year-old, presented a calm, smiling face upon our meeting. Unlike a number of children, who wanted to look out of a window to see if they could see their homes, David seemed immediately secure in his new surroundings. He asked questions concerning the nature of the study, more to satisfy his natural curiosity than to alleviate any discomfort caused by a new situation.

David's play scenarios depict a family orientation of reasonable openness. Parent dolls and child dolls enjoyably interact, but the child miniatures also spend time pursuing their own areas of interest. The little boy is immersed in reading an adventure story. When we later progress to questions of belief, David rapidly and comfortably circles "believe very strongly" and offers, "I enjoy thinking about God and how we can know God exists." Still later, when asked about learning, he al-

ludes to finding out about what to read at school but
then spontaneously expands on this response:

> I read and think a lot on my own. This is important
> to me. [DH: What is important?] God. Thinking
> about God. I want to know more about what God is
> like. I try to ask a lot of people, and read . . . and I
> try to figure things out.

What seemed to stand out about David was his pleasant and sincerely trusting demeanor and, equally striking, his ardent faith. David clearly believed there was
something "out there," "in there," or just "there"—
some God that David, like a religious Christopher
Columbus, wished to discover and explore.

Family Problems as a Distorting Influence

As this discussion of trust suggests, aberrations or
difficulties in family relations will change and color the
development of a child's personal faith. It is most difficult for a child saddled with overbearing family problems and perhaps with resulting neuroses to confront
the question of a God's existence. In corresponding
manner, open self-explanation is precluded or clouded
by personal difficulties.

Problems weigh heavily on a small person's mind and
create tremendous interference and tension concerning
spiritual development. Several of the children painfully
illustrate how family discord or insensitivity can profoundly influence the course and nature of their deity
representations.

Ten-year-old Annette, whose drawing appears in
chapter 7, came to her interview under the most unfortunate of circumstances. As this petite girl walked
through the door with her mother, several drops of
blood were streaming down from her nose and threat-
ening to seep into her mouth. As I later discovered,
Annette had fallen an hour earlier while roller skating

and for some inexplicable reason, her mother had not immediately attended to her injury. Suppressing any distress or fear, Annette remained stoic. Once I gave her a cloth and some ice, she assured me that she was ready to begin. I asked her mother why she had let Annette go, and she merely replied that she was afraid of being late. In contrast to her interviewer, Annette seemed to be taking the episode in stride. It was readily apparent to me that negligence in parenting was something Annette was familiar with.

As one might anticipate, Annette's conception of a deity was harsh and overbearing, demonstrating little helpful involvement in her everyday life. Her drawing graphically underscored this point. Overall, Annette conveyed the sense that she thought that there might be some good deity somewhere, somewhere over the rainbow, but she experienced little in a heartfelt way about this possibility. Her faith was weak, too long muddled by the vast neglect in her young life. "Maybe there is a God," Annette seemed to say, "but it must be someone else's God."

Annette's play scenarios represent rote descriptions of biblical stories, which she emphasizes are very distant to her. In the family doll scene, mother and father periodically scold the little girl as "the Lord" stands passively by. In the "child alone" play action, the traumatic events of the day make their way into story form. The little girl runs in a frightened manner from the possible dangers of the forest. The Lord only watches. At the scene's conclusion, the little girl stoically thanks the Lord for "giving her enough energy to run away from any pain there might be." Clearly, Annette's troublesome family circumstances, as highlighted by one painful afternoon interlude, seem centrally involved in the creation of a distant and unhelping deity. From my vantage point, it seemed that it would have required unparalleled personal strength for her to imagine anything different.

The relevance of such family troubles speaks to the commonly noted relationship between personal difficulty and religious belief, as Freud emphasized. However, in listening closely to Annette and some of her peers, to explain all religious belief as an artifact of neuroses goes much too far. It is a highly generalized conclusion based on a part of the puzzle of spiritual development. Certainly, family and paternal images infuse God representations. Yet, as we have suggested with the presentation of the children's common themes, such familial imagery, however recalcitrant, eventually seems to dissipate. In addition, no one has satisfactorily explained why negative God imagery persists in the inner worlds of the healthiest of individuals. What all this suggests is that a direct and personal relationship between a child and his or her God conception may indeed be tenable, and this conception can extend beyond family-filtered or family-related concerns.

The Necessity of Individuation

Separating from the parents of childhood and becoming a person in one's own right is a fundamental task for the child-turned-adult. Individuation is a natural process that is essential for personal growth. Correspondingly, individuation also emerges as a necessary step in free and unencumbered religious exploration.

While a child or adult may appear independent in their religious outlook, as perhaps occurs with the practice of atypical rituals or the overt expression of unusual beliefs, what is crucial is the presence of inner emotional independence. The child must detach from the expectations, patterns, and internalized images of parents. The individuation must be thorough, regardless of the parents' view, and the child must remain open to the natural vicissitudes of life. For some children, as well as adults, the process may never be concluded, and they will wander on a labyrinthian path—a path made even more difficult by stagnating early family and socialization influences. For more fortunate youngsters, the process of religious individuation is rendered possible by a facilitating background, though the process itself is never guaranteed and never facile.

An important aspect of religious individuation seems to be a certain tolerance of aloneness. The children who demonstrate a comfort in being alone, as well as a joy in being with people, also display highly individualized and original deity conceptions. "Time alone" seems to allow a child to develop his or her own beliefs outside of a parental shadow, however benign that parental oversight might be. A few children in particular, representing all three age groups, seem to think seriously about the world and themselves during intervals of aloneness. I focus on one of the older children because she is among the most fluent in describing her discoveries.

Portions of twelve-year-old Tamara's interview have already appeared in relation to prior subjects, but some of her responses are well worth reconsidering in the context of individuation. Tamara's entire protocol was quite thoughtful and her family scenarios were most revealing. In these scenarios, we trace the experiences of the little girl doll. The small character does not seem unhappy or filled with tension about other family members, but her attention is clearly placed on seeking out new adventures for herself. In the words of Tamara, "The girl is interested in learning about herself, deciding what she would like to be in life." In the "parents alone" segment, Tamara discusses the parent dolls but offers a split-stage effect, notifying her audience that the little girl is writing in her diary about her ambitions. Next, in the "child alone" scenario, the relation-

ship between the little girl's solitude and her deity
becomes clearer. As Tamara describes,

> She isn't as interested in imaginary friends, like
> some kids might. She wants to get closer to God,
> because she believes God is real. Afterward, she
> will talk to her parents about her wish to be closer
> to God and they will be supportive.

It seems that Tamara is beginning to conceive of a
direct and personal relationship with her God. While she
brings in the parent dolls at the conclusion of the last
scenario (some degree of acceptance is still important to
her), she seems to be just outside of the realm of
parental permission. She is beginning to be her own
clergy. While Tamara introduces this personal relationship with a God during her interview, her responses,
like those of many of the other children, indicate that
she is not yet prepared to embrace this relationship
fully. However, she does seem to be moving steadily
toward a mystery that awaits her.

The Child's Discovery: God and Self

As we have seen in the discussion of common themes,
now and then the children seem to find their way to
their deeper thoughts and feelings, and thus to a more
spontaneous and original God of their own. As we look
closely, the children show a growing sense of a distinct
"self," an individual thinker who has left behind parental interpretations and parental imagery. While no specific child demonstrates a thoroughly individuated
sense of self, many of the children manifest occasional
breakthroughs. It is perhaps most accurate to say that
the children have moments of a "newborn God," a God
beyond apparent socialization influences.

These moments carry with them a special quality.
The children seem to speak with an air of authority; if
not actually possessing some truth, they certainly

sound as if they do. At such moments, the children convey a more tranquil sense about the world and about themselves. They intimate a belief in a "just world," not always with the explicit mention of a Creator. As seven-year-old Hallie comments,

> It does not always seem like everything in the world is fair. But you can't always tell by just looking at first, I think. In the end, things work out to be fair.

Above and beyond this, the discovery of one's own efficacy seems to accompany the discovery of one's own God. No longer are the children perceiving themselves as pleasant puppets of the adult world. They seem to believe that they can have great impact on the world. Certainly, they continue on with many unanswered questions about their God. They take with them, however, a natural appetite for meaning and great taste for the freedom to explore.

─── 10 ───────────────

Epilogue: For Children Only?

Dear God,
Thanks for the memories. I realize that it
is now too late to become a guard for the
Celtics, but there are other things I want to
do . . . like winning a Pulitzer Prize, for
example. How about some help?

David

Children's conceptions of God are not for children only.
Through their simplifications, children tell us much
about the prevailing concerns and predilections of the
adult world. For every seven-year-old boy who demonstrates a great distance between doll figures and a wish
for God's intervention, there lives a forty-seven-year-
old man who feels detached from his family and conjures
only a distant God. Children invariably become the
adults we know ourselves to be and they bring with
them all of their images, conflicts, and beliefs. Perhaps
Anthony Storr said it most succinctly when he com-
mented, "We are all children, even if most of us have
forgotten it" (1966, 24).

One way to recall and discover one's internal child is
to attempt the play tasks and interview questions. I
sensed a special relationship between the children's
conceptions and adult conceptions when I undertook
the process myself. And, as I quickly learned, if whole-
heartedly entered into, grappling with one's God representation is no easy challenge. There is something in
the nature of this process that not only brings out the

"child" in us, but also brings out the "self" in us. We discover something about who we really are.

A brief reading of my own protocol reveals a thematic panorama similar to the portrait indicated by the children. To my surprise, I could discern the imagery of formal religion, the undeniable socializing stamps of a Jewish childhood and a Catholic education. Less startling were the many hallmarks of age. Most notably, my mid-twenties investment in "becoming my own person" seemed to find its way into the deity conception; it overshadowed any remnant of adolescent themes or any precursors of middle-age motifs. And, lo and behold, I report with mild chagrin that my God was a thoroughly active fellow, and we can underscore "fellow." But the traces of a romanticized notion of a divine relationship were perhaps even more apparent. In my personality-dominated conception, my lovers in heaven rendered the characters of the Song of Solomon and *Love Story*, even if considered collectively, comparatively platonic and passionless.

Family influences were similarly unmistakable. Father, mother, and my "wished-for" and "feared images" all appeared in at least cameo roles. Frequently, I oscillated between familial images as a way of not relinquishing any of them. Yet I wanted to enter a more original and more unexplored inner world.

Themes such as "transformation" and "connectedness" are emergent as well, distinguished by the very unorthodox but prevalent manner in which they are woven into my thoughts. Perhaps because socialization is so pronounced and long-standing for the adult, basic themes run further from the surface of our everday lives. And yet, if we look and listen carefully, the motifs of "transformation" and "connectedness," for example, are with us all the time, as is clear in my response to the question about God's everyday activities:

The spirit of life is like the meeting of a taxicab and

us, the passengers. We wait anxiously at the curb, hoping to flag down the vehicle. We fear that others will get there first, or even if this is not the case, that we and the driver will somehow not see each other.

Alas, we see the vehicle and it sees us. It stops for us. We get in, hurriedly and yet tentatively. The ride continues. We traverse city streets and sidewalks that we didn't even know existed. We bask in the glory of each red light successfully anticipated and, at the same time, wonder to ourselves if we are traveling too fast.

More suddenly than we anticipate, we reach our destination. As the door lies open for us, we realize that this journey was indeed quite expensive. We are befuddled that a simple ride could cost so much. Silently, we gaze upward at the tall city building. Indeed, we've reached our destination and that's what seems to matter. We've arrived. But we are again surprised. Amidst our anticipation and our relief, we are incessantly preoccupied with the feeling that we have somehow been here before.

Children, too, who know little of taxicabs and urban driving, seem to have their own journeys to distant and apparently unknown cities. Through their God representation, the children teach us much about the world and about our beliefs concerning the world. They tell us that the world has a personality all its own, filled with joy and pleasure. They demonstrate to us that the world is vastly complex; it presents constant socialization and at the same time it calls for great spontaneity. The children intimate to us that the world is filled with contradictions, not the least of which is faith and doubt in a deity. And the children seem to say, "If in reality there is a deity," and they seem to whisper that there is, "then it may well turn out to be the Children's God."

Appendix: The Children's Interview

Part 1: Naming the Deity
 Directions: When you think of what best represents
  your own beliefs about life, what word or words
  would you use to describe the most important
  thing in your beliefs?
Part 2: Drawing the Deity
 Directions: Now I want you to imagine what (child's
  name for deity) would look like if you pictured
  _____ in your mind. If this is hard to do, or you
  don't usually picture _____ in this way, please let
  me know.
Part 3: Storytelling about the Deity
 Directions: Now, could you tell me a story about your
  picture? Just make one up and answer these questions: What is going on in the picture? What are the
  characters thinking and feeling? What led up to
  this? What will happen?
Part 4: Playing the Deity (Family Scenarios)
 Directions: Next, I have here a small family of dolls
  and I want you to imagine a family situation—any
  family situation. But with this family, I want you
  to play _____. I want you to show me what, if
  anything, _____ would do or say with such a family.
  You can act how you like.
 Scenario 1: The entire family and _____
 Directions: Here is the first situation. There will be
  two others (child is given all five dolls).
 Scenario 2: The parents and _____ alone
 Directions: Here is the second scene (child is given
  two adult dolls).

Scenario 3: The child and ____alone

Directions: Here is the last scene. I want you to choose one of these three dolls (points toward three child dolls) to be alone with ____.

Part 5: Questions and Answers about the Deity

A. Description of the Deity

　1. Description

　　Directions: Could you describe in words, using one word or many, what ____ is like?

　2. Home of the Deity

　　Directions: How, could you tell me, where do you think ____ lives? Is ____ alone there? What is ____'s home like?

　3. Sex of the Deity

　　Directions: Now, could you tell me what sex ____ is, if you think ____ has a sex? How would things be different if ____ had a sex (or was the other sex)?

B. Activities of the Deity

　1. Activities

　　Directions: First, can you tell me what ____ does, if anything, that involves the everyday activities and concerns of people like you and me? How is ____ involved?

　2. Hurt and Troubles

　　Directions: Does ____ have something to do with things that hurt or with troubles that people have? If so, describe one. How is ____ involved?

　3. Fun

　　Directions: Does ____ have something to do with things that are fun, enjoyable, or make you feel good? If so, describe one. How is ____ involved?

　4. Birth

　　Directions: Now I want to ask you about

some'special kinds of events. When someone
like you is born, is _____ involved? If so, how?

5. Death: Older Person

Directions: When someone like a grandma or
grandpa dies, is _____ involved? If so, how?

6. Death: Younger Person

Directions: When someone young dies, like
from an accident or from a disease, is
_____ involved? If so, how?

C. Belief in the Deity

1. Belief

Directions: First, I'd like to know how much
you believe in the _____ you just described.
I'm interested in how much you believe in
general, even if you aren't sure of a few
things:

a. a whole lot

b. pretty much believe

c. sometimes or kind of believe

d. don't really believe

2. Strong Belief

Directions: Can you remember a time or period
of your life that you believed very strongly,
perhaps when something important hap-
pened?

3. Strong Doubt

Directions: Can you remember a time when
you were strongly doubtful or unsure about
your belief, perhaps when some other significant thing was happening?

D. Feelings about the Deity

1. General Feelings

Directions: Can you tell me how you feel about
_____ most of the time?

2. Specific Feelings

Directions: Now, I'm curious about some specific feelings. Ever feel surprised or amazed

about ____? Sorry or guilty toward ____?
Happy about ____? Sad about ____? Scared
of ____? Angry at ____? Ever feel love for ?

E. Communication with the Deity

1. Conversations

Directions: Is it possible to have a conversation
with ____? How is it possible to let
____ know about something?

2. Questions

Directions: Are there questions that you would
like to ask ____ if you could? Is there something that you're particularly curious
about?

3. Changes

Directions: Are there things you would like to
change about ____ if you could? Make believe that you are a special kind of helper
and that you can give ____ advice.

4. Learning

Directions: Where did you learn about
____ from? From anyone in particular?
From any ways that don't involve other
people?

5. Versus Other Group Members

Directions: How do you think the way you see
____ might be different from other people's
ideas at (name of religious site).

6. Versus Parents

Directions: How do you think the way you see
____ might be different from your parents'
ideas?

F. The Deity and Famous Figures

1. Deity and Familiarity

Directions: I'd like you to tell me whether
____ is as real, more real, or less real for you
than:

a. Santa Claus

  b. E.T.
  c. President Reagan
  d. your daddy
  e. your granddaddy
  f. your great-granddaddy
2. Deity and Similarity

   Directions: Now, I'm going to say come other names. This time I want you to tell me in what ways _____ is similar or different from the following. Please choose any three of these names:

   a. Jesus
   b. Mary
   c. Ghandi
   d. Moses
   e. Mohammed

Part 6: Letter to the Deity

   Directions: Last, I would like you to do a little writing. I'd like you to try to write a letter or note to _____. Perhaps you've done something like this before? Well, just include anything you'd like to say and anything that you think is important that we did not talk about.

References

Allport, Gordon. 1955. *The Individual and His Religion.* New York: Macmillan.

Bardwick, Judith. 1971. *Psychology of Women.* New York: Harper and Row.

Beauvoir, Simone de. 1968. *The Second Sex.* Trans. H. Parshley. New York: Knopf.

Bednarik, Karl. 1970. *The Male in Crisis.* New York: Knopf.

Belgum, David. 1963. *Where Religion and Psychology Meet.* Englewood Cliffs, N.J.: Prentice-Hall.

Bertocci, Peter. 1971. Psychological Interpretations of Religious Experience. In *Research on Religious Development*, ed. M. Strommen. New York: Hawthorn Books.

Bettelheim, Bruno. *The Uses of Enchantment: The Meaning and Importance of Fairy Tales.* New York: Knopf, 1976.

Blume, Judy. 1970. *Are You There, God? It's Me, Margaret.* New York: Dell Publishers.

Buber, Martin. 1964. "The Eternal Thou." In *Philosophy of Religion*, ed. John Hick. Englewood Cliffs, N.J.: Prentice-Hall.

Chasseguet-Smirgel, Janine. 1970. *Female Sexuality.* Ann Arbor: University of Michigan Press.

Chrenka, Rosalyn. 1983. "Fantasy: The First Five Years." Manuscript, University of Michigan.

Clark, Walter. 1971. "Intense Religious Experience." In *Research on Religious Development*, ed. M. Strommen. New York: Hawthorn Books.

Coles, Robert. *Children of Crisis. Vol. 1.* Boston: Little, Brown, 1964.

Dennis, Wayne. 1966. *Group Values through Children's Drawings.* New York: John Wiley and Sons.

Descartes, René. 1958. Philosophical Writings. Selected and translated by Norman Kemp Smith. New York: Modern Library.

Dixon, C. Madelaine. 1930. *Children Are Like That.* New York: John Day Company.

Eastman, Theodore. 1982. *The Baptizing Community.* New York: Seabury Press.

Elkind, David. 1971. "The Development of Religious Understanding in Children and Adolescents." In *Research on Religious Development,* ed. M. Strommen. New York: Hawthorn Books.

———. 1978. *A Sympathetic Understanding of the Child.* Boston: Allyn and Bacon.

Erny, Pierre. 1973. *Childhood and Cosmos.* Washington, D.C.: Black Orpheus Press.

Erikson, Erik. 1964. *Childhood and Society.* New York: Norton.

Fackenheim, Emil. 1970. *God's Presence in History.* New York: New York University Press.

Fairchild, Roy. 1971. "Delayed Gratification: A Psychological and Religious Analysis." In *Research on Religious Development,* ed. M. Strommon. New York: Hawthorn Books.

Ferguson, John. 1980. *Greek and Roman Religion.* Park Ridge, N.J.: Nayes Press.

Fowler, James. 1981. *Stages of Faith.* New York: Harper and Row.

Freud, Sigmund. 1933. *New Introductory Lectures on Psychoanalysis.* Standard Edition 22. New York: Modern Library.

———. 1937. *The Future of an Illusion.* Standard Edition 21. New York: Modern Library.

Fynn, J. 1974. *Mister God, This is Anna.* New York: Ballentine Books.

Garvey, Catherine. 1977. *Play.* Cambridge: Harvard University Press.

Glazer, Nathan. 1957. *American Judaism.* Chicago: University of Chicago Press.

Godin, André, and Hallez, Marthe. 1964. "Parental Images and Divine Paternity." In *From Religious Experience to a Religious Attitude,* ed. A. Godin. Brussels: Lumen Vitae Press.

Goodnow, Jane. 1977. *Children's Drawing.* Cambridge: Harvard University Press.

Gosse, Edmund. 1909. *Father and Son: A Study of Two Temperaments.* London: Heinemann.

Greeley, Andrew. 1977. *The American Catholic.* New York: Basic Books.

Harms, Edward. 1944. "The Development of Religious Experience in Children." *American Journal of Sociology* 50:112–22.

Havighurst, R., and Keating, B. 1971. "The Religion of Youth." In *Research on Religious Development,* ed. M. Strommen. New York: Hawthorn Books.

Heirich, Max. 1977. "Change of Heart: A Test of Some Widely Held Theories about Religious Conversion." *American Journal of Sociology* 83:3.

Heller, David. 1982. "Themes of Culture and Ancestry among Children of Concentration Camp Survivors." *Psychiatry* 45:247.

Jung, Carl. 1938. *Psychology and Religion.* New Haven: Yale University Press.

Kierkegaard, Søren. 1946. *A Kierkegaard Anthology.* Ed. Robert Bretall. Princeton: Princeton University Press.

Kirkhart, Robert, and Kirkhart, Elizabeth. 1972. "The Bruised Self: Mending in Early Years." In *The Child and His Image.* Boston: Houghton Mifflin Company.

Klein, Carole. 1975. *The Myth of the Happy Child*. New York: Harper and Row.

Klepsch, Marvin, and Logie, Laura. 1982. *Children Draw and Tell*. New York: Brunner-Mazel.

Küng, Hans. 1979. *Freud and the Problem of God*. New Haven: Yale University Press.

———. 1981. *Does God Exist?* New York: Vintage Books.

Kushner, Harold. 1981. *When Bad Things Happen to Good People*. New York: Schocken Books.

———. 1971. *When Children Ask about God*. New York: Schocken Books.

Lederer, Wolfgang. 1968. *The Fear of Women*. New York: Grune and Stratton.

Lefevre, Paul. 1963. *Understandings of Man*. Philadelphia: Westminster Press.

Lewis, C. S. 1966. *Of Other Worlds*. New York: Harcourt Brace Jovanovich.

Lips, Hilary, and Colwill, Nina. 1978. *The Psychology of Sex Differences*. Englewood Cliffs: Prentice-Hall.

Machover, Karen. 1949. *Personality Projection in the Drawing of the Human Figure*. Springfield, Ill.: Thomas.

McMillan, Carol. 1982. *Women, Reason, and Nature*. Princeton: Princeton University Press.

Malinowski, Bronislaw. 1955. *Magic, Science, and Religion*. Garden City, N.Y.: Doubleday.

Mann, Richard. 1984. *The Light of Consciousness*. Albany: State University of New York Press.

Marshall, Eric, and Hample, Stuart. 1966. *Children's Letters to God*. New York: Simon and Schuster.

———. 1967. *More Children's Letters to God*. New York: Simon and Schuster.

Martin, J., and Westie, F. 1972. "The Tolerant Personality." In *Prejudice in Children*. Springfield, Ill.: Thomas.

Marty, Martin. 1971. "Religious Development in Historical, Social, and Cultural Context." In *Research on*

Religious Development, ed. M. Strommon. New York: Hawthorn Books.

———. 1972. *Protestantism.* New York: Holt, Rinehart and Winston.

Moody, Raymond. 1976. *Life after Life.* Harrisburg: Stackpole Books.

Nelson, Michael, and Jones, Edward. 1957. "An Application of the Q-Technique to the Study of Religious Concepts." *Psychological Reports* 3:293–97.

Nietzche, Friedrich. [1888] 1974. *The Gay Science.* Trans. W. Kaufmann. New York: Random House.

Otto, Rudolph. [1923] 1958. *The Idea of the Holy.* London: Oxford University Press.

Piaget, Jean. 1969. *The Child's Conception of the World.* Totowa, N.J.: Littlefield, Adams and Company.

Rahner, Hugo. 1967. *Man at Play.* New York: Herder and Herder.

Redl, Fritz. 1951. *Children Who Hate.* Glencoe, Ill.: Free Press.

Rizzuto, Ana-Maria. 1979. *The Birth of the Living God.* Chicago: University of Chicago Press.

Rubenstein, Richard. 1976. *After Auschwitz.* Indianapolis. Ind.: Bobbs-Merrill.

Rubin, Zick. 1980. *Children's Friendship.* Cambridge: Harvard University Press.

Sartre, Jean-Paul. 1948. *The Emotions: Outline of a Theory.* Trans. Bernard Frechtman. New York: Philosophical Library.

Smith, Wilfred. 1962. *The Meaning and End of Religion.* New York: New American Library.

Shorey, Paul. 1903. *The Unity of Plato's Thought.* Chicago: University of Chicago Press.

Spilka, Bernard. 1971. "Research on Religious Beliefs: A Critical Review." *Research on Religious Development,* ed. M. Strommen. New York: Hawthorn Books.

Stace, Walter. 1952. *Time and Eternity.* Princeton: Princeton University Press.

Steinberg, Milton. 1947. *Basic Judaism.* New York: Harcourt Brace Jovanovich.

Steward, Charles. 1967. *Adolescent Religion.* New York: Abingdon Press.

Stoller, Robert. 1972. "The Bedrock of Masculinity and Femininity: Bisexuality." *Archives of General Psychiatry* 26:207–12.

Storr, Anthony. 1966. *The Worlds of Children.* Ed. Edward Blisher. London: Hamlyn.

Strunk, Orlo. 1959. "Perceived Relationships between Parental and Deity Concepts." *Psychological Newsletter* 10:222–26.

Suransky, Valerie. 1982. *The Erosion of Childhood.* Chicago: University of Chicago Press.

Ulanov, Ann. 1981. *Receiving Woman: Studies in the Psychology and Theology of the Feminine.* Philadelphia: Westminster Press.

Vanden Burgt, Robert. 1981. *The Religious Philosophy of William James.* Chicago: Nelson-Hall.

Weisz, John. 1980. "Autonomy, Control, and Other Reasons Why Man Is the Greatest: A Content Analysis of Children's Mother's Day Letters." *Child Development* 51:801–7.

Wolfenstein, Martha. 1965. *Children and the Death of the President.* Garden City, N.Y.: Doubleday.

Young, Arthur. 1976. *The Reflexive Universe.* Boston: Merloyd Lawrence.

Zablocki, Benjamin. 1971. *The Joyful Community.* Baltimore: Penguin Books.

Zeligs, Rose. 1974. *Children's Experience with Death.* Springfield, Ill.: Thomas.

Index

DATE DUE